PRAISE FOR

HAIL, HAIL, EUPHORIA!

"*Hail, Hail, Euphoria!* is the most lyrical, insightful, scholarly, illuminating, and celebratory one hundred forty-four pages I've ever sat down with. This book is a stream of fun."

—*Wall Street Journal*

"Roy Blount Jr. deconstructs the Marx Brothers' magic."

—*Los Angeles Times*

"An essential read for Marx Brothers fans, those curious about the melding of war and humor in film, and browsers looking for a good read."

—*Library Journal*

"Roy Blount Jr. knows from humor. In *Hail, Hail, Euphoria!*, he sets out to remedy the lack of a scene-by-scene commentary on the Marx Brothers' greatest movie, the sublimely nonsensical *Duck Soup*."

—*Washington Post*

"Readers will enjoy the stories behind this iconic film and the careers of the Marx Brothers."

—*Booklist*

ALSO BY ROY BLOUNT JR.

HAIL, HAIL, HAIL,

PRESENTING

THE MARX BROTHERS

IN

DUCK SOUP,

THE

GREATEST

WAR MOVIE EVER MADE

EUPHORIA!

Roy Blount Jr.

itbooks

AN IMPRINT OF HARPERCOLLINS PUBLISHERS

*it*books

A hardcover edition of this book was published in 2010 by It Books, an imprint of HarperCollins Publishers.

HAIL, HAIL, EUPHORIA! Copyright © 2010 by Roy Blount Jr. All rights reserved. Printed in the United States of America. No part of this book may be used or reproduced in any manner whatsoever without written permission except in the case of brief quotations embodied in critical articles and reviews. For information address HarperCollins Publishers, 10 East 53rd Street, New York, NY 10022.

HarperCollins books may be purchased for educational, business, or sales promotional use. For information please write: Special Markets Department, HarperCollins Publishers, 10 East 53rd Street, New York, NY 10022.

FIRST IT BOOKS PAPERBACK PUBLISHED 2011.

Designed by Sunil Manchikanti

The Library of Congress has catalogued the hardcover edition as follows:

Blount, Roy.

Hail, hail, euphoria! : presenting the Marx Brothers in Duck Soup, the greatest war movie ever made / Roy Blount Jr. — 1st ed.

p. cm.

ISBN 978-0-06-180816-6

1. Duck Soup (Motion picture). 2. Marx Brothers. I. Title.

PN1997.D845B57   2010

791.43'42—dc22

2010021740

ISBN 978-0-06-180817-3 (pbk.)

11 12 13 14 15   OV/RRD   10 9 8 7 6 5 4 3 2 1

For Pauline Kael

HAIL, HAIL, EUPHORIA!

It will come to this.

Imagine you belong to a savage yet sophisticated cult, which goes way back before your time even, and you haven't attended an observance for a while. And you hear that an introductory service is to be held, and when you walk in, there are all these *children* there, and their young, earnest, probably over-parenting parents or over-nannying nannies are there, and you think, Oh my gods (this cult is polytheistic), these *newbies* are going to be humming along off-key and clapping on the beat, they're going to be going *Wha?* at all the philosophical moments and hissing the sacrifices—or worse, they'll be getting off on it all in some trashy, prurient, mocking way. They're going to walk all over my heaven, trampling the lush undergrowth, and then they're going to walk out and leave me sitting here cursing and sobbing into my hands.

Such was my anxiety recently as I sat in Symphony Space's Thalia Theater in Manhattan before a daytime screening of *Duck Soup*. The Thalia is where I saw that movie for the first time, fifty years ago. Back then, the Thalia was cramped, ratty, mildewy, and darkly over-intellectual inside, and I can't begin to tell you how much I, a lank youth up from Georgia, loved it. Now the Thalia is cheerfully refurbished. (A revival house? Quaint notion.) *Duck*

Soup isn't refurbished. Parents were shushing the offspring whom they had dragged to this *old black-and-white* . . .

I was sitting next to this one six- or seven-year-old, Theo, who was trying to hustle another kid's mother into getting out of there with him (and, presumably, her kid) and going back to her place for a playdate. "We're doing this, the movie, instead," she said. "No, this isn't *playing*," he said.

But then the movie started. The audience blinked at *Duck Soup* a few times, and then they laughed, readily, steadily, sliding along with *Duck Soup* like Harpo in white socks on a polished floor. Some of the kids looked frankly amazed. Okay, these were New York City kids. But when was the last time you saw kids—*especially* New York City kids—looking amazed? At something done by men in their forties, seventy-seven years ago? Even Theo, after a little while (the entrance of Vera Marcal perked him up, but I think it was Groucho singing with his pants rolled up that got him), was into it.

You know that scene in *Sullivan's Travels* where Joel McCrea watches a Mickey Mouse cartoon with fellow members of the chain gang and their raucous laughter convinces him that comedy-making is worthwhile? The laughter at this screening of *Duck Soup* was of a better quality than that. It was also better than what I hear in theaters today in response to either of the extremes of contemporary not-for-kiddies comedy. It was better, that is, than the rank, startled barking you hear at a Borat or Brüno gross-out.* And better than the shallow upchuckly sound of an audience somehow vaguely gratified by the schlubby spectacle of guys getting in touch with each other's feelings, the genre that has come to be called bromance.

---

* Harpo gets in bed with a horse, sure, but he would never tongue kiss one, as Chris Kattan has done in a recent yuk-fest.

Duck Soup was getting family laughs, but edgy. Vintage laughs, but fresh. Even the parents seemed to have come unprepared for this movie. They looked too young to have been aware of *Duck Soup* when it was widely revived and became a big hit, for the first time, in the sixties. "Groucho's mustache wasn't real?" I heard one mother ask another after the screening. "It looked like just a piece of felt." It's *greasepaint,* for Godsake, it's unreal, like everything in this anarchic, farcical—

> **CHICO:** What'samatter you? 'At's-a no farcical. No wheels.
>
> Wheels?
>
> **CHICO:** Two wheels, you got a bicycle. Three wheels, you got a tricycle. Four wheels, then you got a farcycle.
>
> I see, I see—
>
> **CHICO:** Nahhh—i-c-i-c, 'at's-a spelling icicle. Hey, I got a riddle for you. What is it has got two Eskimo brothers, they look just-a like him? Give up? An icicle— he's a frozen driblet.
>
> You take a special interest in native Alaskans?
>
> **CHICO:** Nahh. I'm not all that Inuit.

I have worked and worked on that, and, I know, it's labored. For Chico, puns are duck soup: "A nice, cold glass eliminate." It's partly in the writing, but it's mostly in how he puts them across. What moved those parents and children most, I think, was how the people in that old movie move. Like when Harpo dances in the tank of nice cold eliminate. And especially when two or three or four Marx brothers are moving together.

Duck Soup doesn't have everything. "If you asked me to name the best comedies ever made," Woody Allen said in an interview, "*Duck Soup* is the only one that really doesn't have a dead spot."*

It doesn't have a romantic subplot either. For Groucho or Harpo or Chico—or even Zeppo, in this movie—to "get the girl" onscreen would be like a dybbuk getting a job. The brothers make eyes at girls, and Harpo chases them, but they get only Margaret Dumont, who is tolerable because she doesn't get them. When *Duck Soup* came out, audiences across America failed to get it. It didn't make much money—partly because there wasn't much money in 1933, but also because *Duck Soup* didn't mirror the national mood. It may not mirror the national mood now. It doesn't care. It mirrors something more primal. Something heedless and ruthless as kids playing war.

I don't want to oversell it. In London in 1931, Thomas Wolfe wrote to a friend in the States that he dreaded going with his swellegant English publishers to see the Marxes onstage. "I suppose I shall have to listen to the usual horrible guff . . . 'You know there's Something Very Grand about them—there really is, you know, I mean there's Something Sort of Epic about it . . . I mean that man

* Aside from the one joke that has died, as we shall see.

who never says anything is really like Michael Angelo's Adam . . . you know they are really *Very* Great Clowns, they really are, you know,' etc. etc. etc. ad vomitatum."

There is no vomiting in *Duck Soup*. There are no poop jokes. (An outhouse joke in the script was replaced by a doghouse joke.) The Marxes violate personal boundaries without resorting to naked wrestling or talking penises.

There is only one thing *Duck Soup* lacks and might be said to need: a commentary track. On the DVD there are no special features except subtitles in Spanish and French. Only once that I know of* has this movie been accompanied by a running interpretation. Groucho, in his eighties, watched *Duck Soup* at home one evening with Marvin Hamlisch's attractive young sister, Terry, whose relationship with Groucho extended to big, sloppy, sort-of-tongue-in-cheek, so to speak, kisses. The two of them were "kinda necking in the dark," as Ms. Hamlisch told Charlotte Chandler, a chronicler of Groucho's dotage. "The lyrics, the songs, the numbers and everything, he remembered how each thing was shot. He got so excited, he almost broke my knee in the dark, which was a big thrill."

I can't match that, and Terry Hamlisch is no longer living to recall it. But I've got *Duck Soup* up on the upper left corner of my computer monitor here, and I can fill you in on some background as we watch it together. I may even toss in some dead spots.

And if you must have romance:

"My parents met," says Jane Stine of New York City, "while backing away from *Duck Soup*." Not recoiling. Retreating, slowly,

---

* Unless you count the Woody Allen character in *Hannah and Her Sisters* working out a reason not to shoot himself while watching the "Freedonia's Going to War" scene, which we will come to.

reluctantly, up the theater aisle after having already, separately, sat through *Duck Soup* twice. Tearing themselves individually away from *Duck Soup*, that's what brought them together. Their eyes, full of Marxes, met. And they knew.

Maybe the Marxes were funnier in their younger days, when various combinations of them were a vaudeville act, presided over by their mother, Minnie Marx. When they made *Duck Soup*, they just had to compete with the Great Depression, *King Kong*, and the rise of Fascism. In vaudeville they had to stand out among Collins and Hart, who had a cat that blew a whistle; "The Musical Cow Milkers," a husband-wife team who sang while she, in a pinafore and sunbonnet, milked a live cow; and Mons Herbert, whose act, according to Harpo, was "playing 'The Anvil Chorus' by blowing knives and forks against each other. For a finish he would blow up a prop roast turkey and deflate it in such a way that it played 'Oh, Dry Those Tears' out of its rump." Not to mention Swain's Rats and Cats. (The rats rode the cats.)

In those days the brothers had to suppress their animal spirits. Mother Minnie kept an eye on them from the wings. She made sure they behaved—put on a good safe musical act with traditional comic turns—by shouting "Greenbaum." That was the name of the man who held the mortgage on the family home. But when Minnie wasn't looking, they would improvise. Groucho singing "La donna e mobile" accompanied by Chico on piano could become, in Harpo's recollection, "a six-hand, three-key version of 'Waltz Me Around Again, Willie'—Chico on the stool, me sitting on Chico's shoulders, and Groucho crouching behind us, reaching his arms around Chico like tentacles, and all of us singing." Follow *that*, Mons Herbert.*

We do know that in l933, the depths of the Great Depression, *Duck Soup* was regarded in the industry as too funny for its own good. Since then, Samuel Beckett has stolen hat gags from it for *Waiting for Godot*. Gene Kelly, Bugs Bunny, and many others have been inspired by it. In 2009 an international panel of critics voted *Duck Soup* the thirty-seventh greatest film of all time, and yes, it is the movie that makes the Woody Allen character in *Hannah and Her Sisters* decide not to shoot himself.

It's not just a Marx Brothers movie; it is also a Leo McCarey movie. That dashing, conflicted Irish-American Catholic was the only inspired director they ever worked with. In other Marx movies, a dumb romantic story was wedged in, for the ladies. McCarey ruled that out for *Duck Soup*. It could be that he didn't want the Marxes bursting in and out of his own subtle way of conveying romance. On the whole, he hated working with them.

Jean Renoir, whose own touch was light, said of McCarey, "He understands people—better perhaps than anyone else in Hollywood." Faint praise perhaps. But here is a quite sensible but somehow magical exchange from another movie directed by McCarey, *Ruggles of Red Gap*.

---

* The closest thing to this in any of the brothers' movies is one of the few high points of *The Big Store*, in which Harpo and Chico play their only filmed piano duet, and they do some rumba moves together, while playing, and then Harpo is banging the keys from behind Chico, through his legs, and then Harpo is on Chico's back . . . This was supposed to be the brothers' last movie. At the beginning of the duet, Chico says to Harpo, "You remember I used to give you lessons," which in fact his mother told him to do in their boyhood and which he did, if at all, only perfunctorily. Pretty much anything a Marx brother ever learned, he figured out for himself.

ROLAND YOUNG (playing an English earl who is so cool his lips barely move): Do you believe in love at first sight?

LEILA HYAMS (playing the beautiful proprietor of a sort of G-rated bawdy house in Red Gap, Washington): No.

YOUNG: No, neither do I. That's why I'd like to stay around for a while.

In a scene set up by McCarey and improvised by the actors, Leila tries to teach Roland to play the drum. The most nearly passionate word in it is "ditta-boom." Gets me every time. Check it out on YouTube. There's another moment in *Ruggles* between Charles Laughton, the gentleman's gentleman whom the earl loses (Ruggles, that is, was the stake) in a poker game, and Zasu Pitts—I'll tell you about it later.

Ruggles is also the only unabashedly patriotic movie—except for *Yankee Doodle Dandy*—that I would ever recommend. Charles Laughton reciting the Gettysburg Address in a cowboy bar . . . it gets you. If in *Duck Soup* the Gettysburg Address had ever come up, it would have been pelted with fruit. The closest thing to romantic in *Duck Soup*, Jane Stine's parents' reaction to it aside, is Groucho's eagerness to marry, for her money, the woman he relentlessly insults.

McCarey was a bit of a rounder, but also devout and sentimental. The last two qualities must have had some impact on *Duck Soup*, but it's hard to see where. *Duck Soup* doesn't have a reverent or softhearted bone in its body. It tells how a band of brothers—that is to say, three maniacs (and Zeppo, a maniac's secretary)—take over (*relevance alert*) a bankrupt nation and, while constantly mocking and sabotaging everyone, including each other and themselves, lead that nation giddily into war.

Didactic is another kind of bone *Duck Soup*'s body doesn't have. "It kidded dictators," McCarey once said. As we shall see, there is more to it than that. W. H. Auden once wrote that Iago, in *Othello*, was driven by "motiveless malignity." *Duck Soup* perpetrates motiveless indignities. It is sheer . . .

Let's watch it.

The first bird you see is not a duck. It's an eagle. Why an eagle? Try rallying a nation around a duck. President Franklin Delano Roosevelt was freshly elected and had a big majority's hearty, not to say desperate, mandate. "The whole country is with him," said Will Rogers. "If he burned down the Capitol, we would cheer and say, 'Well, we at least got a fire started, anyhow.'" But FDR couldn't make this eagle fly. This eagle was killed by a sick chicken.

It's the NRA blue eagle, symbol of the National Recovery Administration, which was created the year *Duck Soup* came out. Banks, farms, factories, mills, and mines had failed. Twenty-five percent of workers were unemployed, and in 1933 "workers" mostly meant "men," so if the man of the house was laid off, the household was hungry. And in 1933 there were no food stamps, no aid for dependent children. No deep-pockets China either. People were riding the rails, living in packing crates, standing in line for hours to get free bread.

People well established in entertainment did better than others. Groucho had been wiped out by the stock market crash in 1929 and claimed he didn't get a good night's sleep thereafter for the rest of his life, but Hollywood and radio had replenished his coffers. When Harpo's margins were starkly exposed by the market collapse, "[I] liquidated every asset I owned except my harp and my croquet set," and he still had to come up with $10,000 to avoid utter ruin. Zeppo saved him. Stop moping, Zeppo said, and come with me to a gambling boat, and be sure to bring some burnt cork. I urge you to read that story—nothing to do with blackface—in Harpo's autobiography, *Harpo Speaks!*

In real life, of course, Harpo did speak. At first he spoke onstage, presumably in an Irish accent since he played a dumb Irish type generically called Patsy Brannigan. He went mute after Uncle Al Shean forgot to write him any lines in a new sketch for the family act, and Harpo said, Okay, I'll ad-lib, and he did, and next day in the papers his ad-libs were panned. So he stopped speaking professionally, even when interviewed on radio (he would honk his horn) or TV. In *Raised Eyebrows: My Years Inside Groucho's House,* Steve Stoliar writes that while working for Groucho as an archivist, he did find a note that in 1940, when the brothers were trying out their *Go West* routines onstage, Harpo, after being applauded for his harp solo, stepped forward and delivered a long speech concluding as follows: "May I not have the rather unusual privilege of tending to you, my audience, the warm congratulations which are rightfully yours for the keenness and perspicacity which you have shown in recognizing true genius, accomplished artistry, and monumento-monumania. Thank you."

Somewhere along in there Groucho shouted, "Now you know

why he never talked!" In January 1963, at a fund-raising concert for symphony orchestras at the Pasadena Civic Center, Harpo took the stage to announce his retirement and then, as Simon Louvish puts it, "he astounded and delighted his audience by talking at great length, unleashing a stream of tales and anecdotes that seemed to be never ending. Then he walked off the stage forever." He died the following year.

One audio clip of Harpo speaking has survived. It may have been recorded while he was working with his collaborator on *Harpo Speaks!* You can hear it at www.marx-brothers.org/biography/bbc2.wav. In a surprisingly adult-sounding soft baritone, he tells about the time he fainted off the piano stool twice while playing in a whorehouse, because he had the measles, and the madam had him thrown out, saying, "I don't want any sick Jews around me." He was just a kid when that happened.

"We Do Our Part" it says there under the NRA eagle. For the Marx Brothers, that meant making this insane movie. "If you think this country's bad off now," as Groucho sings, "just wait till I get through with it." What FDR did, in his first year as president, was to push through Congress a flurry of programs called WPA, CCC, TVA, SEC, AAA. People called them his "alphabet"—

> **CHICO:** 'At's-a no good.
>
> **GROUCHO:** What? The alphabet? Is no good?
>
> **CHICO:** 'At's-a right. You got somebody over here, wanna make a bet, that's halfabet. Somebody

over here, wanna take a bet,
that's another halfabet. 'At's-a
no good. You gotta get in a
whole bet.

GROUCHO: The next time you get
in a hole, remind me to leave
you there.

FDR's "alphabet soup," those programs were called. Some of
them helped a lot and are still with us today, but not the National
Recovery Administration. The NRA enjoined the nation's indus-
tries to develop self-regulatory codes of "fair practice," designed to
create better working conditions, new jobs, and mercantile enthusiasm. The NRA's director, and *Time*'s Man of the Year 1933, was
the former army general Hugh "Iron Pants" Johnson. Johnson delivered this message to "chiselers" and "rugged individualists" who
refused to rally behind the NRA:

> Away, slight men! You may have been leaders once. You are
> corporals of disaster now and a safe place for you may be
> yapping at the flanks but it is not safe to stand obstructing
> the front of this great army. You might be trampled under-
> foot—not knowingly but inadvertently—because of your
> small stature and of the uplifted glance of a people whose
> "eyes have seen the glory."

Two years later the NRA itself was trampled, by an alleged "unfit
chicken." Joseph, Martin, Alex, and Aaron Schechter ("butcher"

in Yiddish) operated kosher wholesale poultry slaughterhouses in Brooklyn, New York. They ran afoul—

CHICO: Hey, 'at's-a good one!

—so to speak, of the Live Poultry Code. When it came to enforcement, the NRA's eye undertook to be on the individual chicken. Its inspectors came to the Schechters' slaughterhouse and charged them with purveying a questionable chicken, an unhealthy-looking chicken, which is why the matter became known as the "sick chicken case." The NRA inspector, testified Joseph Schechter, was "a very nice boy . . . He don't know from a chicken." The Schechters appealed their conviction all the way up to the U.S. Supreme Court, which rendered the chicken's health moot by declaring the NRA unconstitutional, on broader grounds.

Disillusioned, General Johnson authored a memoir of the NRA's rise and fall, *The Blue Eagle: From Egg to Earth*. Might there have been a Marx Brothers movie in that book, the brothers as the Schechters and Louis Calhern as Iron Pants? No, too reality-bound. The Marxes had once been, as we shall see, chicken *farmers*, but in *Duck Soup* they fly higher than chickens or ducks, off into the empyrean. Transcendent individualists and chiselers they are. Charged with saving a nation from financial disaster.

In *Duck Soup* the blue eagle is not blue. This movie, like all Marx Brothers movies, is in black and white. Flesh tones would not suit them. The only known color footage of the brothers in movie mode is fifteen silent seconds of them rehearsing a crowd scene for *Animal Crackers*. Everyone is in full fancy-dress costume except Harpo, who comes prancing through the throng wearing bedroom slippers and a faded blue-gray bathrobe. No wig. Very little hair. He looks like your cousin Freddy, assuming your cousin Freddy is a highly unexceptional-looking person—except when everybody but Freddy is dressed for a gala and one of Freddy's brothers is wearing a painted-on mustache and eyebrows and another brother is wearing a mop under an elfin pointy hat and he, Freddy, by which I mean Harpo, is in a bathrobe.

"Harpo, we're trying out this new process, just as a test—come on, we're all waiting for you to walk through the scene with us, see it in *living color*," and Harpo shows up as uncolorfully as possible. I was about to say, that's Harpo all over. But Harpo all over

Harpo, Chico, Groucho, and Zeppo, each at a different stage of unreadiness.

would have lost the bathrobe. In all sorts of settings, Harpo took a toddler's delight in popping up in a state of nature. As far as that goes, so did his brothers. During the making of *Room Service,* the Marxes demanded that the set be closed to visitors, but a special party of outsiders was allowed in anyway. In the scene about to be shot, a then-unknown beauty named Lucille Ball was to burst into a room, slam the door, and keep running. She did so. Her pursuers, Groucho, Harpo, and Chico, were to burst in after her. They did so, in the nude. And the visitors were priests and nuns. Back when clergy were a lot more shockable probably.

Another time, as Somerset Maugham was giving a group of guests, including Harpo, whom he had just met, a guided tour of his villa, Harpo dropped back and then reappeared diving naked through the master bedroom window into the pool. Maugham, delighted, disrobed and joined him.

And when the director of *Horse Feathers* couldn't get the crowd he had assembled for a big football scene to show any enthusiasm for the third or fourth take, Harpo said he'd take care of it. He did a lap around the field naked and honking his horn, and the fans went wild.

In the aforementioned silent color clip, Groucho is clearly not delighted by Harpo's appearance. He looks at Harpo askance. Askance was Groucho's attitude toward life. He was born with one eye (or the other one) very slightly awry, so he was never quite—even when directly addressing the camera—looking in only one direction. In a strange humor-analysis book entitled *Enjoyment of Laughter,* Max Eastman maintains that when Groucho "says something, his eyes drop off into the corners of their sockets like those of a doll that you have moved into a horizontal position by accident." This is hyperbole. Groucho's rolled eyes are sentient, cultivated, athletic. One eye, unable to believe what the other eye is seeing, is looking to the viewer, or to heaven (not likely), or to the spirit of Minnie, or, conceivably, to his own inner child (which has been left at his doorstep), as if to say, *Why me? Why you? Why anybody?*

CHICO: Hey, boss, what's-amatter you no make-a the eye contact?

GROUCHO: None of your strabismus.

Der Eifersüchtige (the jealous one) or *der Dunkle* (the dark one) is what their mother called Groucho growing up. In color, he may be wondering how come his older brother gets to be the only one in a bathrobe.

In life, as on the screen, Harpo had already evolved way beyond askance.* Harpo was sillier, simpler, and sweeter than Groucho or than Chico, the oldest.

Chico was their mother's favorite. His birth followed by a few months the death in early infancy of the first child, Manfred. Chico may have felt doted upon for two, beyond his due, so he undercut himself. Or maybe a double load of unconditional love

---

* Harpo told the *Saturday Evening Post* in 1951 that the role he played in *Duck Soup* was his favorite because "Brownie was an even dumber person than I usually play. I love to play illiterate characters. I'm almost one myself, having read only two books in my life, and Brownie was super-illiterate." Two problems with that statement: by 1951 Harpo had in fact become, by many accounts, a keen book reader, and the name of his character in *Duck Soup*—except in certain copyright documents, which do call him Brownie—is Pinky.

made affection so predictable, he had to keep screwing up in order to make things interesting. He spent most of his time losing money on anything but favorites—what's the fun of backing a horse that has any considerable chance to win?—and winning the favors of many, many women (aka chicks), hence his nickname, pronounced *Chick-o*, not *Cheek-o*. In this little clip of color footage, Chico is just standing there, apparently lost in thought. He has more on his mind than moviemaking. He is waiting for a chance to slip away and phone his bookie.

Chico's wife, Betty, did call him *Cheek-o*. Once she urged him to complain to his brothers that they upstaged him and didn't allow him enough screen time. He decided she had a point and went off to argue his case. He returned looking shaken. "You almost broke up the Marx Brothers," he told Betty. The act had room for only two prima donnas, he said. He didn't need to be a star. "I just want the act to work"—so he'd have the wherewithal for his true calling: making merry with money, cards, and the broads, as he had been doing since early-onset adolescence.

The next thing you're going to see is a snow-topped mountain peak surmounted by an arc of stars and the legend "A Paramount Presents Picture." That would seem to be a typo. In all the other Marx Brothers movies for Paramount, the mountain is saying "A Paramount Picture." Maybe this time the boys had the logo rattled.

Not counting an early silent film, *Humor Risk*, which, by all accounts, stank and which has at any rate been lost, Paramount produced the Marxes' first five movies. *The Cocoanuts* and *Animal Crackers* were versions of their hit stage shows, filmed in Astoria, Queens, New York. The Marxes grew up in Manhattan, whence Minnie stage-mothered them into show business.

The brothers were quick to say that none of them would have amounted to anything if it hadn't been for Minnie. "Her doelike looks were deceiving," Harpo says in *Harpo Speaks!*

> She had the stamina of a brewery horse, the drive of a salmon fighting his way up a waterfall, the cunning of a fox, and a devotion to her brood as fierce as any she-lion's. Minnie loved to whoop it up. She liked to be in the thick of things, whenever there was singing, storytelling, or laughter. But this was in a way deceiving too. Her whole adult life, every minute of it, was dedicated to her Master Plan.

That was to make stage stars of her sons. Her brother, Al Shean (born Schoenberg), had achieved a career in song and patter, most notably as half of the comedy team Gallagher and Shean. ("Positively, Mr. Gallagher?" "Absolutely, Mr. Shean.") Uncle Al impressed the boys when he came to visit, wearing matching fedora and spats and handing out dimes. But only Groucho, after leaving school to help support the family, thereby giving up on following in the footsteps of his father's chiropodist, was eager to go into show business. The others, except for Chico, who joined late, were prodded into it by Minnie.

Zeppo, for instance. Zeppo was Buster Marx, a Ford Motor Company mechanic and car thief who carried a gun, when Minnie called and said Gummo had been drafted ("We can do without you," she had told Gummo), so Zeppo had to catch a train right away to Rockford, Illinois, to join his brothers because the act was billed after all as the *four* Marx brothers. Zeppo said, "Ma, I have a date." He didn't mention that it was a double date: he and his tough older friend Louis Bass, who had led him into serious crime (his brothers having been too much older and too far away to be role models), were meeting two girls whom they planned to entertain by taking them into some bushes.

And Minnie said, It doesn't matter, you have to go.

So Zeppo went. And that night Louis Bass met the girls but also their brothers, who were going to beat him up so he shot one of them to death and as a result went to prison for twenty years and when he got out he went into drug dealing and the police came and Bass decided to shoot his way out and he was killed. That's the story Zeppo told, some sixty years later.

But Minnie wasn't trying to save Zeppo from all that; she was just keeping the act together and her word was law, so Zeppo went and when he got to Rockford he didn't know any of the act but he went on anyway and ad-libbed and faked some dance steps and he was an entertainer (four or five shows a day at the beginning there) for the next fifteen years.

As the boys were entering middle age Minnie died—in Harpo's arms, after eating *two* hearty dinners and whooping it up with the boys at table tennis (picture Marx family Ping-Pong!) and having a stroke—four years before *Duck Soup*. In *Harpo and Me,* Harpo described her last moments:

> Then she saw me. She did the hardest thing she had ever done in sixty-five years of doing the impossible: she smiled. Her lips trembled. Her eyes were glazed with fear. But two tiny stars twinkled through the glaze, and she smiled.
>
> The smile went quickly out. Her fingertips fluttered against the bedcover. She was trying to say something.

I knew what she was trying to say. I reached over and straightened her wig, the new blond wig she had bought especially for tonight. The smile came back for a second. Then it faded, and all the life in Minnie faded with it.

In a documentary on the Marxes, Chico's daughter, Maxine, is a cheerful and confident interviewee, but when she remembers what it was like after Minnie passed, her face falls: "All the boys were there. They were seated around the table. I had never seen the Marx brothers as a group that *down*. There was a pall over the room. I was eleven years old, and all I felt was the atmosphere. I looked at them all, and I got out. It was a *terrible* moment."

Early on, Minnie appeared with the boys, in the role of a learning-impaired schoolgirl. It's frustrating not to have any moving, much less speaking, image of her. In still photos she looks a little like Harpo, wig and all, but considerably plumper. (She would arrive at parties laced into a corset, but then, having made her entrance, she would take the corset off.) She insisted on a class act—comedy leavened with unfarcical music. They felt their strengths lay in horseplay, however, and Chico, who was good at making connections, took over the managerial reins when the boys were thirtyish.

Horseplay, musical and non-, made them stars on Broadway. By 1929, wrote Groucho, "we were the toast of the town, which is a lot better than being in a breadline." New York's most stylish literary clique, the celebratedly witty Algonquin Round Table, took Harpo to its acidulous bosom. Not Groucho. Whereas Harpo, at this time, was not even much of a reader, Groucho regarded himself, with reason, as a writer, and he admired in particular the most genial of the Round Tablers, the humorist Robert Benchley. Benchley was a

fan of Groucho's work, but Groucho himself, Benchley told someone, "makes me nervous. He's always on the edge of his seat."

(Harpo, too, was always poised vis-à-vis Benchley but in a different way. According to Ben Hecht, "Harpo would wait for Benchley to fall in love, like a huntsman waiting for a bird dog to flush" a bird, and bingo, the lady in question would end up not in Benchley's arms but in Harpo's—in Benchley's apartment, though, since Harpo had the use of it.)

The Marxes' conquest of Gotham and the commercial and critical success of their first two movies gave them clout. The most lucrative place to throw that clout around was Hollywood. They moved there, permanently as it turned out. They made *Monkey Business* (which, except for its flat ending, is one of their best films) and *Horse Feathers,* both of which were highly profitable. Paramount itself, though, was no healthier than the rest of the nation, and the Marxes decided to go indie. The Four Marx Brothers Inc., with Harpo as titular president, would mount their own project, a movie version of the musical *Of Thee I Sing,* starring themselves.

Of Thee I Sing—a sprightly takeoff on American politics (but with nothing in it as subversive as three choruses of "Hail, Hail, Freedonia, laaaand . . .")—was the first musical to win the Pulitzer Prize for drama. George and Ira Gershwin wrote the music and lyrics, and George S. Kaufman wrote the book and directed. This was the project about which Kaufman made an often-quoted cautionary comment: "Satire is what closes on Saturday night." *Of Thee I Sing* concerns a man who runs for president on a platform of, simply, love. He plans to marry the winner of a special beauty contest and ride that factitious romance into the White House. But real love intervenes. He jilts the beauteous blond contest winner (who vows revenge) for a practical woman who bakes great corn muffins. He is elected, and the first lady will be a cornucopia of muffins to the unemployed.

The complications that ensue amount to a lively tug on America's leg at a time when theatergoers were in need of a lift. But Groucho marrying for corn-muffin love? Or for that matter, love? Chico might have worked as the play's chief justice of the Supreme Court, a muffin-susceptible court that engages in absurdist arguments. But where's the role for Harpo? Is it Alexander Throttlebottom, who keeps trying to get people to notice that he is vice president? Nobody doesn't notice Harpo. So what? Harpo plays the blonde? And Kaufman was not eager to see his play Marxized. He was a friend of the brothers and had written, in collaboration with them and others, the stage versions of *The Cocoanuts* and *Horse Feathers*. Eventually he would be lured to Hollywood to write *A Night at the Opera* for them. But he was an honored and meticulous dramatic craftsman. The story goes that he once interrupted a full rehearsal of *Horse Feathers* to say, "Hey! I think I just heard one of my lines."

To posterity's great relief, the Marxes' *Of Thee I Sing* project fizzled. Then, with only Zeppo at his side, the Marxes' father, Sam, known as Frenchie because he came from Alsace-Lorraine, died. He had been a terrible tailor professionally, a wonderful cook at home. Cheerfully dominated by Minnie when she was alive, he pursued the housemaid later. "Frenchie never stopped smiling, and his smile was like a secret radiation," Harpo would recall. The brothers now were middle-aged orphans. For one more movie, they reconciled with Paramount. A highly unstable combination of people would gather at that pinnacle to help them make their masterpiece.

Fade out mountain, fade in ducks. Four of them swimming and quacking in a big black pot with a fire beneath. Right away, this movie is not cuddly.

So many movies have mice. Mickey, Minnie, Mighty, Stuart Little. Ignatz, whom Krazy Kat dotes on hopelessly, Jerry and Tuffy, whom Tom can never get over on. A Muppet mouse, a Russian immigrant mouse, a French chef mouse (okay, a rat, but a cute rat), an Italian mouse on *Ed Sullivan* (remember Topo Gigio?), city mouse and country mouse, a widowed field mouse named Mrs. Brisby, mice in *Alice in Wonderland* and *Cinderella,* Amos the mouse who tells how he and Ben Franklin discovered electricity. Serpico (like Lenny, unfortunately, in *Of Mice and Men*) has a pet mouse, Dr. Doolittle talks to a mouse, and Stockard Channing refers to "mouse-beds" in *The Fortune.* In l933, when he was nine years old, Billy Barty, the great dwarf actor, played a mouse in a Busby Berkeley number in *Footlight Parade.* Cast the mouse and you got a movie.

Mice you can live with in the house. Ducks, no. According to Helen Lawrenson, a journalist-hottie-about-town in the mid-l930s, one of the fashionable joints in New York was the Chapeau Rouge, whose owner, Pepy d'Albrew, wore a live white mouse in his buttonhole. Not a duck. A duck wouldn't stand for it.

In movies, also, ducks aren't easy. There's Donald, whose chops led the critic Dave Hickey to call him the Dizzy Gillespie of Disney characters, but who is not cool. Donald throws duckfits—jumps up and down and squawks abusively at his nephews (who, being ducks themselves, can handle it). In "Der Fuehrer's Face" (1942), Donald dreams that he has become a Nazi flunky, and it drives him phantasmagorically insane. (A great performance. If only for its bracing lack of subtlety, I put it ahead of Chaplin's in *The Great Dictator*.) Then there's Daffy, who has an exthplothive lithp and when excited goes bouncing around in all directions off all parts of his body and making a variety of *hoo-hoo h'h'hoo oo-h'hoohoo wuh-hoo hw-w'hoo woo* noises. And briefly there was Howard, an extraterrestrial "sarcastic humanoid duck" (to quote imdb.com) who, as a griping, cigar-smoking comic-book hero drew comparison to Groucho. But sweetened up by George Lucas for the blockbuster flop *Howard the Duck,* he became a synonym for turkey.

In *Horse Feathers* there is a duck. It is swimming behind the canoe in which Groucho is serenading the college widow, played by Thelma Todd. As she paddles, Groucho is lying back, singing "Everybody Says I Love You," and accompanying himself on the guitar. Will Rogers once wrote that Groucho could play the guitar as well as Harpo the harp and Chico the piano, "but he never does. So he is really what I call an ideal musician; he can play, but don't." Thelma tries to wheedle something out of Groucho by using baby talk. Not the tack to take with *der Dunkle.* "Is that coming from you, or the duck?" he asks Thelma. She winds up in the water, and the duck with Groucho in the canoe.

Boiling ducks alive, unplucked and swimming, is an impractical approach to soup making. And after these four in the pot (I don't want to dwell on this, but how did they keep them in there? Are they tied by the feet?), no ducks appear in *Duck Soup.* Why, then, the title? Groucho offered this explanation: "Take two turkeys, one goose, four cabbages, but no duck, and mix them together. After one taste, you'll duck soup for the rest of your life." That seems less than dispositive. "Duck soup" is an old American slang phrase meaning something that's as easy as pie, or someone who's a pushover. According to *Duck Soup,* taking over the helm of a bankrupt nation, if you go about it cynically and irresponsibly enough, is a breeze. Everyone is a pushover for the Marxes, and they, to varying degrees, are pushovers for one another.

What kind of statement was this for a movie to make in the depths of the Depression? By contrast, when Barack Obama became leader, more recently, of a nation in danger of going bottoms-up, he said, "Our American story has never been about things coming easy."

Easy, no. Dreamy, yes.

"The Four Marx Brothers," the screen reads next. In a moment we will see duck-bodied caricatures of them popping onscreen in this order: Groucho, Harpo, Chico, and Zeppo. As far as I know, they never had any arguments about billing. It seems natural now for Groucho to come first and then Harpo, but Chico was the eldest, born Leonard in 1887; then Harpo, born Adolph, 1888; Groucho, born Julius, 1890; and Zeppo, born Herbert, 1901. Someone once said Groucho was ego, Harpo superego, Chico id. Or maybe Harpo id, Groucho superego . . . To me, they overlap. But each of them, except for Zeppo, was essential, in life and in art: Groucho the brains, Harpo the heart and soul, Chico the operator.

Everybody, including the brothers themselves, dropped the legal names for the *o*-ones. Chico's, as we have seen, was inspired by his knack with the opposite sex. Harpo (who did the literal chick-chasing onscreen) played the harp, except in *Duck Soup.* Groucho was grouchy, and in the old vaudeville days he carried around his neck what was known in those circles as the "grouch bag," which held valuable articles that might otherwise have been stolen. His name is sometimes said to have been influenced by a comic-strip character named Groucho, but that, like many other possible facts concerning the Marxes, is something of which we cannot pretend to be certain. The origin of Zeppo's name is especially obscure. He was named for the Zeppelin goes one story, for a popular trained chimp named Zippo (he insisted on the vowel change) is another. The one that seems most likely to me is that one morning when the brothers were chicken farmers (as indeed they were, for reasons not unconnected to *Duck Soup*), Herbert called out to Chico, "Hi, Zeke," and Chico replied, "Hi, Zep." A more likely hick name would have been "Zeb," but *Z* was a good initial for Zeppo, the last of the Marxes and the one most likely to put people to sleep.

Backstage Gummo, who would always be the least famous brother, walked quietly, as if wearing gumshoes. He was born Milton in 1892. As a boy, he was part of the vaudeville act only because Minnie dragooned him. He stuttered, but not when he sang, and he was billed as "the world's slowest whirlwind dancer." After his military service, Gummo happily went into the dress business in New York. A. J. Liebling, then reporting for the *New York World-Telegram,* once asked him whether the Marxes were always funny: "I don't know," he replied. "We never gave me a laugh." (What did Liebling expect? "Oh yes, we keep me in stitches"?) When the Depression killed Gummo's dress business, he went out west to handle the brothers' managerial details.

Chico and Harpo (under Chico's tutelage) had survived on the streets as juvenile delinquents, but they were too little to rely upon their fists. If Chico found himself confronted by an Irish gang, he could sound Irish; an Italian gang, Italian. Zeppo was a tough guy who dreamed of being a boxer. Some people said he was the wittiest brother offstage. Once when Groucho got sick Zeppo replaced him

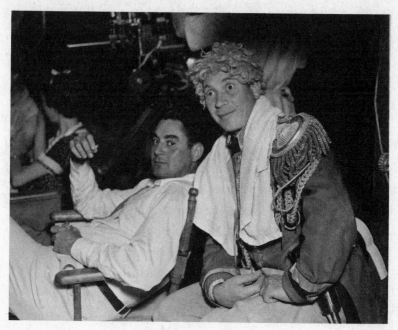

McCarey and Harpo. On the whole, they saw eye-to-eye.

in the vaudeville act, and nobody noticed the difference. Zeppo as Zeppo was, as David Steinberg says, "a lox. But there was a spirit there with the four Marx brothers that wasn't there with the three of them." *Duck Soup* is Zeppo's last movie.

The next thing on your screen is "Directed by Leo McCarey." Directed by, yes. Remembered with pleasure by, no. McCarey had turned down the assignment, in fact, and was about to leave Paramount to make sure he wouldn't have to take on the brothers, but then they left Paramount, so he signed back up with that studio, and then they returned, "and I found myself in the process of directing the Marx Brothers. The most surprising thing about this film was that I succeeded in not going crazy, for I really did not want to work with them: they were completely mad. It was nearly impossible to get all four of them together at the same time."

McCarey is not often ranked among comedy auteurs like his contemporaries Frank Capra, Howard Hawks, Ernst Lubitsch, and Preston Sturges. But when Capra was breaking into movies at the Hal Roach Studios, "the man I watched the most," he said, "was that handsome, black-haired Irish director, Leo McCarey. The ease and speed with which this young genius cooked up laughs on the spot for Laurel and Hardy made my mouth water."

Stan Laurel was an inspired creator of comic business himself, but he idolized McCarey, who brought Laurel and Hardy together and directed—or "supervised," a term of the silent era that entailed various aspects of conceiving, writing, directing, editing, and producing—most of their great silent films. (One of them was called *Duck Soup*, but no resemblance.) McCarey directed, and largely wrote, movies starring an extraordinary variety of comedians: Charlie Chase in many silent shorts, Eddie Cantor in *The Kid from Spain*, W. C. Fields and George Burns and Gracie Allen in *Six of a Kind*, Mae West in *Belle of the Nineties*, Harold Lloyd in *The Milky Way*. He directed Cary Grant and Irene Dunne in one of the best of all screwball comedies, *The Awful Truth*, and Charles Boyer and Dunne in *Love Affair*, which Michael Sragow has called "the apex of the 'you'll-laugh-you'll-cry' kind of movie." McCarey did the remake too, *An Affair to Remember*, with Grant and Deborah Kerr, and the Oscar-winning churchy-weepy comedy *Going My Way* with Bing Crosby and Barry Fitzgerald. And as I mentioned, McCarey directed *Ruggles of Red Gap*.

I say he "largely wrote" those movies, but he was not a writer, he was a talker, "and in a time and place where there was a paucity of readers and a plethora of listeners, talkers were more effective (and more successful) than writers," writes Garson Kanin. In his memoir, *Hollywood,* Kanin recounts a pitch McCarey made to Samuel Goldwyn and staff.

Goldwyn was desperate for someone to come up with a project for Gary Cooper and Merle Oberon. Without letting on that he was aware of this, McCarey mentioned that he had a story idea. Goldwyn summoned all his people to his office to hear McCarey tell it. To those people's astonishment, McCarey stretched out on Goldwyn's sofa, paused for effect, and began to talk.

The male lead, McCarey said, "is a cowboy . . . the manliest, sexiest, bravest, ballsiest son of a bitch you could ever imagine . . .

"Now, *wham!* Cut to Saturday night." A dance hall. McCarey vocalized what the band was playing. "Cowboys dancing with cowboys . . . That's what I used to do when *I* worked the ranch. And I don't think anybody ever expected *me . . .*"

Indeed, McCarey was a well-known ladies' man. As Elsa Lanchester puts it in her memoir, *Elsa Lanchester Herself:*

> McCarey . . . had a weakness for pretty women and always fell in love with them. He told Charles [Laughton, her husband,] he deeply regretted this, as he had a wife and daughter and didn't want to hurt them. "But," as he said to Charles, "here I am sitting opposite a girl in the commissary and I find myself saying to her, 'You eat your lettuce so pretty.' I'm in love and I can't help it."

Back to McCarey's pitch. The main cowboy is "maybe—well, I don't know . . . as I think about the story, the image I get in *my* mind, is somebody like say—well, say—*Gary Cooper.*"

Goldwyn, Kanin writes, "nodded gravely."

Then another *wham*, and McCarey cuts—humming his own new, higher-toned musical accompaniment—to the ballroom of a la-ti-da eastern finishing school, "uppercrusty girls" dancing with each other. And we close on an especially beautiful dancer. "Somebody beautifully spoken. This is for the contrast . . . Maybe somebody English? I don't know. Maybe there isn't *anybody*. Maybe this whole idea stinks. Wait a minute! I'll tell you who could do it. *Merle Oberon! . . .*

"Oh, by the way, did I tell you the title? No? Get this. Gary Cooper and Merle Oberon in . . . *The Cowboy and the Lady*."

Goldwyn is hooked, and McCarey proceeds, recalls Kanin, "to recite routines, not necessarily in dramatic or chronological order. Some of them could be visualized and were, indeed, entertaining. Others were unclear. All were finally punctuated by McCarey shouting, 'They'll piss! I tell you, they'll piss!' "

The next day Goldwyn bought the story for $50,000 (the equivalent today of a quarter million). That meant McCarey had to write it down, and all he could remember were a few flashes. He talked Kanin into putting on paper as much of it as he could remember, for $500. The resultant outline was not impressive. But Goldwyn forged ahead with the project. When he called McCarey to ask if he would direct the picture, McCarey said, "What makes you think I would want to spend my valuable time on a piece of crap like *The Cowboy and the Lady*?"

When he did commit to a movie, McCarey would rework the script and then gather his cast around a piano and spend most of the day noodling on the keyboard and working out how to improvise the next scene. This procedure made Cary Grant feel so insecure on the set of *The Awful Truth* he tried to get out of the picture. But Grant derived some of his movie-persona coolness from mannerisms of McCarey.

So why didn't McCarey do any acting himself? Elsa Lanchester:

> Leo McCarey was very much in demand after *Ruggles of Red Gap*. He even appeared in person on the *Kraft Cheese Radio Show* to plug the film. He was to just say hello and a few words about the picture. Charles and I had been on the *Kraft Show* and were delighted to get the big basket of mixed cheeses that they gave all guests. Well, Leo was an extremely shy man but full of charm, with an apologetic smile that would melt an agent's gut. But he was terrified into absolute silence when he got to the Kraft microphone. He tried to talk and stuttered, then very rapidly blurted out on the air, "For Christ's sake, give me my cheese and let me go home!"

According to Bob Thomas's biography of Harry Cohn, *King Cohn*, this is how McCarey made *The Awful Truth*. McCarey was unemployed because his sad movie about old age, *Make Way for Tomorrow*, which he always regarded as his best and about which Orson Welles said, "It would make a stone cry," had not made money.

Harry Cohn was the despotic head of Columbia Pictures. He called McCarey up and offered him a property he owned, a script developed from a play called *The Awful Truth*. McCarey read it and went to Cohn's office with his agent. McCarey said he didn't like it but would direct it. His agent asked for $100,000. Cohn said absolutely not.

On his way out of Cohn's office, McCarey noticed a piano. He sat down and played "Down Among the Sheltering Palms." In his youth, as a song plugger, Cohn had gone around to music stores singing and playing that song. Cohn sang along with McCarey and agreed to McCarey's fee.

McCarey threw away the script and sat with a writer named Vina Delmar in a car parked on Hollywood Boulevard, working up scenes.

Actors had already been engaged: Irene Dunne, Ralph Bellamy, Cary Grant. They couldn't make heads or tails of their characters from the bits of script that came to them from McCarey. When Dunne and Bellamy showed up for the first day of shooting, Mc-Carey asked Dunne, "Can you play the piano?"

"Not very well," she said.

He asked Bellamy, "Can you sing?"

"Not a note," said Bellamy.

"Good," said McCarey. He told Dunne to play "Home on the Range" and Bellamy to sing it. And he turned on the camera.

That scene in *The Awful Truth* establishes without a word of exposition that the two of them mean well but are not made for each other. Other scenes were filmed in pretty much the same way. The actors weren't sure what they were doing. Cohn showed up on the set and raised hell. McCarey went home and demanded that Cohn apologize.

Cohn *never* apologized. Once he described his infallible sensitivity to a movie's quality as follows: "If a picture is great, see, I don't move at all. If a picture is good, I just move a little. If a picture stinks, my ass wiggles all over the chair."

Herman Mankiewicz, who had just taken a much-needed job

at Cohn's studio, couldn't resist: "What makes you think your ass is wired to a hundred and forty million other American asses? Where is it written that you've got the monitor ass of the world?" Cohn went apoplectic and fired Mankiewicz. But he was too deeply invested in *The Awful Truth* to fire McCarey, so he returned to the set and tendered an apology.

On the thirty-seventh day of shooting, Cohn returned to the set once again. McCarey was passing drinks around to cast and crew. Cohn exploded.

McCarey told him to calm down: "We're finished." Ahead of time and well under budget. McCarey won an Oscar for *The Awful Truth*. Dunne and Bellamy were nominated. Grant wasn't, but this is the movie in which he came into his own. And McCarey told Cohn to kiss off thenceforward. *That* was how McCarey thought a movie should be made. "And what also pleases me," he told *Cahiers du Cinéma*, "is that it told, somewhat, the story of my life (don't repeat it: my wife will want to kill me . . .). But the few scenes turning on the question of unfaithfulness, I should hasten to say, were not at all autobiographical: my imagination alone is responsible." Right.

McCarey and the Marxes misbehaved in different ways. McCarey, whose father had been a boxing promoter and whose drinking buddies included John Barrymore and W. C. Fields, was a two-fisted carouser. According to a story that sounds like something from a John Ford movie, McCarey and three friends—the writer Gene Fowler and the directors Gregory La Cava and Raoul Walsh—once stood back-to-back-to-back-to-back in a gambling hall and handily trounced a dozen rough customers who objected to their cavalier attitude toward roulette. The Marxes, for their part, were no pushovers. Once when a theater owner refused to pay up (it had been as Minnie warned—they had improvised too merrily) and pulled a blackjack on them, they pulled their own blackjacks and faced him down. But the Marxes drank scarcely at all and did not get into barroom brawls. What they would do—well, Groucho once interrupted a charity tennis match between himself and Charlie Chaplin by spreading out a picnic lunch on the court and eating it as Chaplin fumed. Harpo would pick the pocket of another guest at a garden party, count the money, slip the wallet back into the guest's pocket, and then bet the guest a hundred dollars he could tell him exactly how much money he was carrying. Chico had to go on the lam sometimes when he owed too much money to the wrong people.

The Marxes were laws unto themselves. They were glad to be working with a director they considered classy, but they were not to be gathered around a piano for long—unless as a family, in which case they would be whooping, not musing. An extemporaneous director is not likely to be charmed by actors whose notion of duck soup makes his look like pulling teeth. And yet, they made this wanton soup together.

Jewish-Irish soup, we might say. In the first half of the twentieth century, hyphenated Americans were far more distinctly, even blatantly, ethnic than today, in society and in popular culture. On Broadway the comedy *Abie's Irish Rose,* in which a Jewish boy's marriage to an Irish girl causes repercussions on both sides of the family, ran from 1922 to 1927. It made sophisticates shudder. As drama critic for the old humor magazine *Life,* Robert Benchley came up with a new terse dismissal of the play in every issue.

"America's favorite comedy, which accounts for the number of shaved necks on the streets."

"Contest for best line closes at midnight . . . At present, Mr. Arthur Marx [that would be Harpo] is leading with 'No worse than a bad cold.'"

"See Hebrews 13:8." (If you don't have a Bible handy, the text is "Jesus Christ the same yesterday, and today, and forever.")*

But Jews and Harps together resonated—as potentially attractive opposites perhaps—in a country of immigrants. *Abie's Irish Rose* became a successful movie in 1928 and a radio show and a movie remake in the forties. "For years," recalled the screenwriter-director-producer Nunnally Johnson, "there were more Goddamned Jewish-Irish romances" being written for the stage. "Everybody thinking it's going to have another five-year run. It must have broken a hundred angels." In 1972–73 the Abie-and-Rosemary story was revived in the TV series *Bridget Loves Bernie*. But ethnic assumptions had become less popular. *Bridget Loves Bernie* generated so much controversy and hate mail that CBS pulled the plug on it, making it the highest-rated TV show ever to be canceled. Meanwhile, *All in the Family,* which first appeared in 1971, was thriving and continued to do so until 1979, perhaps because the ethnicities of Archie Bunker and his liberal-opponent son-in-law were unspecific. But those parts, played by Carroll O'Connor and Rob Reiner, respectively, owed a great deal to Irish and Jewish

* In one of the movies a quasi-legal Groucho-Chico exchange ends in Chico explaining "Habeas Irish Rose."

stereotypes. Archie lived in lace-curtain Queens, and the show was created by Norman Lear.

Crudely stereotypical as it is, the meme of Irish and Jewish polarity lingers. "The Jews have guilt, the Irish shame." "Ireland sober would be Ireland free, or at least much more Jewish." In political entertainment in recent years we have had Al Franken and Jon Stewart, on the one hand, and Bill O'Reilly and Sean Hannity, on the other. But except for Mel Brooks and Tom Meehan (*The Producers, Hairspray*) in the theater and Ben Stiller (son of the comedy team Stiller, Jewish, and Meara, Irish) in movies, we don't have the creative Hebrew-Hibernian hybrids that used to abound in popular culture. Besides the aforementioned Gallagher and Shean (the latter originally Schoenberg), we once had the marriage—on vaudeville, radio, and TV and in real life—of George Burns and Gracie Allen; the mock radio feuds ("Benny couldn't ad-lib a belch at a Hungarian banquet") between Fred Allen (born John Florence Sullivan) and Jack Benny (Benny Kubelsky); and the byplay among Benny and his sidekicks Phil Harris and Dennis Day. In the theater, George M. Cohan and Sam H. Harris were longtime partners. John O'Hara and Gene Kelly got together with Richard Rodgers and Moss Hart to create *Pal Joey,* and Kelly and Stanley Donen did *Singin' in the Rain.* Then there were the three Jews, Yip Harburg, Fred Saidy, and Burton Lane, who celebrated Irish mythology in *Finian's Rainbow.*

American literature has produced no single Jewish-Irish character as juicy as James Joyce's Leopold Bloom, but in *The Great Gatsby,* by the Irish-American Scott Fitzgerald, "the narrator is horrified and amused," as Adam Gopnik has put it, "by the Jewish gangster Wolfsheim, and toys with and hints at the idea, never quite firmed up, that James Gatz/Jay Gatsby is not just linked to

Jews but is Jewish himself." Norman Mailer's swaggering Sergius O'Shaughnessy strenuously, finally, brings Denise Gondelman to orgasm in "The Time of Her Time." The late Frank McCourt often claimed his next project would be, to quote the *New York Times,* "a bodice-ripper about Mordecai O'Callaghan, the nonexistent first Jewish Irish pirate on the high seas."

As to business, Joseph Kennedy in the twenties said, "Look at that bunch of pants pressers [which was to say, Jewish men] in Hollywood making themselves millionaires. I could take the whole business away from them." Between 1926 and 1930 he took over three studios. He managed, barely, to escape with his pants.

The last woman in Groucho's life, when he was in his eighties and she half a century or so younger, was named Erin Fleming. He made her his secretary and personal manager and expressed his regret, to most anyone who would listen, that he was too old to have sex with her. When he was dying, a terrible legal struggle arose between Ms. Fleming and Groucho's son, Arthur, which she lost, but in happier days she had converted to Judaism. Groucho joked that he was going to become a Catholic and change his name to "the Reverend Patrick O'Hoolihan."

Then there is the case of *Duck Soup*'s producer, Herman Mankiewicz. *Duck Soup* has enough elements in common with *Million-Dollar Legs,* the W. C. Field vehicle that Mankiewicz had produced the year before (it too was set in a mythical kingdom, Klopstockia), that we may assume Mank at least tossed ideas into the hopper during script development meetings, but at some point during the shooting of *Duck Soup* he was fired. He had supervised *Horse Feathers* and *Monkey Business* and would contribute to the screenplay of the classic *Dinner at Eight* and share an Oscar with Orson Welles for the writing of *Citizen Kane*, which is widely regarded as the greatest movie ever made. But Mank was forever shooting himself in the foot. He was, if anything, even less of a respecter of persons than the Marxes—he didn't have much good to say for, or to, them. When Harpo, who had temporarily let his reviews go to his head, asked to see the script of *Monkey Business* so he could find his character, Mankiewicz said his character was "a middle-aged Jew who picks up spit because he thinks it's a quarter." What he lacked was the Marxes' self-preserving canniness. When asked, in 1969 by Tom Stempel, why Mankiewicz had such a checkered career in movies, Nunnally Johnson (whose mother was Irish) replied:

> There was a comedian named Ted Healy. He was an Irishman that had been playing in Shubert shows and vaudeville . . . [Healy] drank with Mank when Mank was at Paramount . . . But Mank said, "I never felt that we were really in sync though we got along very well. Then one afternoon we were having a few."
>
> Healy looked at him for a minute, completely illuminated. He said, "I've got it."
>
> Mank says, "What?"
>
> "I cannot be happy with a fellow till I've got him pegged. Now I've got you pegged."
>
> Mank says, "Well what is it?"
>
> He says, "You're an Irish bum." Perfect description of Mank. He was Jewish, but he was an Irish bum.

Note that Mankiewicz had told this on himself. He was a vainglorious underachiever, generally drunk and always broke (from gambling mostly—he admitted to being "a well-known pigeon") and in need of a loan. After writing for the *New York Times* and the *New Yorker*, he'd been among the first of the Algonquin crowd to go Hollywood, back before sound. (One of his assignments was writing the inter-titles for the silent version of *Abie's Irish Rose*.) He wired his friend Ben Hecht to come join him: "Millions are to be grabbed out here and your only competition is idiots." Driving to a Hollywood party down a steep downhill street and happening to catch a policeman's eye, he lifted both hands from the wheel, cried, "Look! No hands!" and totaled his new car against a telephone pole.

He was witty, though. When a friend asked him, "How's Sara?" he looked puzzled. "Your wife, Sara," said the friend.

"Oh, you mean *poor* Sara," said Mankiewicz.

She was a devoted wife, and he doted on her to the point of soppiness, but jokes trumped sentiment. When a friend came to their house to announce that he'd sold an original script for big money, Mankiewicz turned to Sara and said, "Dance for the gentleman."

Mankiewicz attended a formal dinner party given by a socially pretentious producer named Arthur Hornblow Jr., who liked for everything to be just right. Mankiewicz got so drunk that he threw up. In such a situation, many people would be mortified, and indeed the host and the other guests were stunned. But Mank—no more mortified than he apparently was, deep down, all the time—saw the moment as an occasion to reassure his host. "That's all right, Arthur," he said, "the white wine came up with the fish."

So he wasn't too *refined* for the Marxes. Bert Kalmar is quoted as saying of Mank, "To know him was to like him. Not to know him was to love him." But it may have just come down to this: who needed another jack-of-all-supervision when they had McCarey, who could hold his liquor?

And who was Bert Kalmar? He and his partner, Harry Ruby, as you can see on the screen, are credited with writing the story, music, and lyrics of *Duck Soup*. Ruby, over the years, was probably Groucho's closest friend. Wherever Ruby walked, he kept his eyes to the ground, looking for lost change. He found quite a bit over the years. "It's all profit," he pointed out. "No overhead."

Kalmar and Ruby contributed to other screenplays, but they were primarily songwriters: Kalmar the lyrics, Ruby the tunes. To *Animal Crackers* they had contributed "Hooray for Captain Spaulding" ("the African explorer—did someone call me *schnorrer*?"), which introduces Groucho's character, and "Hello, I Must Be Going," which keeps Groucho's character spinning. In the fifties and early sixties, the tune to the former number would be the theme music for Groucho's radio and then TV quiz show, *You Bet Your Life*. For *Horse Feathers,* Kalmar and Ruby had written Groucho's statement-of-principle song, "Whatever It Is, I'm Against It." And they wrote the absurdist novelty song "Show Me a Rose," which Groucho loved to perform in person. A number of Kalmar and Ruby's love songs became standards: "Three Little Words," "Everyone Says I Love You," "Nevertheless (I'm in Love with You)," "A Kiss to Build a Dream On," "Who's Sorry Now?" and "I Wanna Be Loved by You (Boo-Boop-a-Doo)." In 1950 Warner Brothers turned out a biopic, *Three Little Words,* with Fred Astaire as Kalmar and Red Skelton as Ruby. In this movie they have a falling-out that is similar to the international one that we will come to in *Duck Soup*. They resolve their falling-out not in war, however, but in a song.

Those "additional dialogue" credits, to Arthur Sheekman and Nat Perrin, recognize gag men who contributed to several of the Marxes' movies. In 1934 Sheekman would marry actress Gloria Stuart. They stayed married for forty-four years, until Sheekman's death. In 1998, at the age of eighty-eight, after portraying a one-hundred-year-old survivor in *Titanic*, Stuart was named one of the fifty most beautiful people in the world by *People* magazine. Perrin gave Groucho credit for giving him a start in show business and remained a friend until Groucho died. Sheekman and Perrin apparently helped rework the Kalmar-Ruby script extensively, but such fingerprints as they may have left have long faded away.

Enough with the ducks and the credits—we're in Freedonia! Cozy-looking, pointy-roofed little land nestled in mountains.* But all is not well with the commonweal. Its economy is dowager-based, and you know how that goes—you get $20 million from a dowager and you've got to have more, you're addicted, you've got a dowager jones.

> **CHICO:** Watch-a the puns. Before you know it, you got a punsy scheme.

Erwin Panovsky, the German iconologist, said this about the movies: "Whenever . . . a poetic emotion, a musical outburst, or a literary conceit (even, I am grieved to say, some of the wisecracks of Groucho Marx) entirely lose contact with visible movement, they strike the sensitive spectator as, literally, out of place." Mc-

---

* In some enchanted clime far, we may assume, from Pasadena. That city's Arbor Mansion and Arden Villa, however, provided suitably palatial locations for *Duck Soup*, as they would many years later for the TV show *Dynasty*.

Carey felt the same way about Groucho's punning. In fact, he told *Cahiers du Cinéma* that *Duck Soup* was "the only time in my career, to my knowledge at least, that I made the humor rest with the dialogue: with Groucho, it was the only humor you could get." That is just wrong: Groucho in those days was—as we shall see once we get going in the actual movie here—an eloquent mover, from his greasepaint-enhanced eyebrows to his journeyman-dancer's feet. It is true that Groucho, with or without gag writers, could sparkle verbally. And although McCarey was credited with being a great wit in his day, there is scant evidence of that in surviving records. His remarks in *Cahiers* read as though they were translated into French and back into English (which they may have been). In the interview with him that Peter Bogdanovich did for his book *Who the Devil Made It,* McCarey was limited by severe emphysema, but even so, he sounds less witty on the page than one would hope. He is said to have gone around on the set of *Duck Soup* proudly trying out a line he had come up with—"They fought this war with laughing gas!"—on everyone he came to until finally giving it up. And consider this recollection in the Bogdanovich interview:

> I always remember the time I met Deborah Kerr in Madrid and she said, "Do you remember the dialog on the bridge? 'Winter must be very cold for those who have no memories to keep them warm, and we have already missed the spring.' Do you remember that, Leo?" I said, "Of course, I stayed up one whole night writing that line."

The memory-within-memory of "no-memories" may be appropriate, since the line in question appears in *A Night to Remember,* but Groucho might well have wisecracked that that line's spring had sprung.

So McCarey's contributions to *Duck Soup* were conceptual and visual. "Study the stuff that McCarey made," said his friend and admirer Howard Hawks, "and you'll find that it didn't depend on words, it depended on something that was funny to look at."

Which didn't mean playing with the camera. I know you are eager to get on with the show, but I neglected to mention the credit "Photographed by Henry Sharp." Cinematographer Sharp worked on 117 movies and TV shows between 1920 and 1959. None of them has gone down in history as being of purely cinematographical interest. Irving Pichel, who directed some pretty good movies, once pointed out that in McCarey's *The Bells of St. Mary's* (another Bing-as-priest flick, this time with a demure Ingrid Bergman* as foil instead of Barry Fitzgerald), "the camera is moved not more than half a dozen times—only when it is panned, as the spectator might follow with his eyes a character moving purposively from one part of the scene to another." Nunnally Johnson said McCarey's "camera technique was to tell the actors, 'If you want to be in the movie, get in front of it.'"†

---

* Ingrid on Leo: "I couldn't believe how full of ideas he was. You couldn't *not* like him. If you didn't like him, there was something wrong with you."

† Later, McCarey could use a camera nimbly. In *An Affair to Remember,* Deborah Kerr's character (Terry) doesn't want Cary Grant's character (Nickie) to know that the reason she didn't show up to meet him was that an accident rendered her paraplegic. But Nickie suddenly suspects. As Chris Fujiwara notes in *Defining Moments in Movies,* "He crosses the vast Cinemascope living room, the camera following him, and opens the door to Terry's bedroom. McCarey cuts to a close shot inside the bedroom, where Nickie sees the painting on the wall—proof that Terry was the wheelchair-bound buyer of whom he was told by his gallery owner. Because the camera is on him as he enters the room, we first see his face as understanding dawns on it, and only then does McCarey pan slightly to frame the painting reflected in a mirror. This simple camera movement is a heart-wrenching double-whammy moment of pure cinema."

In previous movies, the Marxes, accustomed as they were to doing the same material onstage, had been hard to corral within the frame. The only filmed example of Harpo's celebrated stolen-silverware-pouring-from-his-sleeve gag scarcely registers, in *Animal Crackers*, for that reason. Even in their later years, the brothers were elusive on-camera as well as off. Eddie Buzzell, who directed *At the Circus* and *Go West*, said:

> They never hit the spots they are supposed to in a moving shot . . . It isn't that they don't know any better or are not co-operative. It's just that their comedy is spontaneous . . . The camera boys tell me they once tried to solve the problem by using three cameras. One was supposed to stay with Harpo, another with Groucho, and a third with Chico, but the names confused them, and when the rushes were shown, they had all "caught" Harpo.

In *Duck Soup* they stay on-camera. They know McCarey is not going looking for them.

Heaven knows *Duck Soup* is not static. It "flows," as Robert Frost said a poem should, "on its own melting." Like a dream, and you know how it is when you try to tell someone your dream the next morning, it's so hard to recapture the flickering images—

> **CHICO:** You can't get-a the flash-a-back.

> Exactly, or to put it another way—

CHICO: Anh-anh-anh . . . Once a pun at a time.

Okay, here we go. Once upon a time there lived a rich widow, Mrs. Gloria Teasdale, played by the monumentally fluty (surely vocal tones such as hers gave rise to the vernacular term "highfalutin") Margaret Dumont. For *Monkey Business,* Groucho had decided she wasn't needed, but he has admitted his mistake and she is back. Here she is confronting the Freedonian government: a bunch of over-dressed old men who want her to lend them another $20 million. (So they can lower taxes, they say. Right.) The man she addresses as "Your Excellency" is, I believe, the one listed as "Zander" in the credits, and portrayed by Edmund Breese, who in this same year was Doctor Wong in *International House.* (No, he doesn't look very Chinese here, but when he faces the camera we can see that he had heavy lids, which with makeup assistance enabled him to take on several Asian roles.) This Excellency will have to go, Mrs. T tells all the old farts, because the government has "beeeen mis*mehn*naged." She has already lent them "mooorr than hoff" of her late husband's fortune, and they have blown it. In return for future investment, she demands fiscal responsibility, by which she means . . .

Here we make a leap. She means that Rufus T. Firefly must become the nation's leadah.

Why do we go along with this? I hesitate to raise such an issue in the midst of a leap, but right here is where our disbelief throws up its hands, and attention must be paid. I assume you are watching *Duck Soup* on your computer monitor, as I am. (Talk about a leap! Technology today! Watching a movie on one corner of a screen while typing away in the middle of that same screen. Oh, I dare say that within a few years you'll be able to *insert yourself into the movie* while you watch it. Don't screw it up.)

Okay. Rewind just a little bit to where we close on Mrs. Teasdale as she is saying:

And now, you're asking for another twenty mill-i-on dollars.

Freeze it! Hold her right there. Groucho isn't the only eye roller in *Duck Soup*. She will be buffeted and disdained in this movie, by diminutive men who in real life have already done things like take her clothes off in a Pullman car and, on another occasion, undress a porter and toss him into her Pullman berth. But she will not

The wealthy benefactress.

show it. She is unlike their mother, in that Minnie would be wearing a wig more or less like Harpo's and would be just about to take off her corset at this point—but she is as buoyant as Minnie, as formidable, and as essential.

How often do things happen because of Logic as opposed to how often because of Presence? Regard Mrs. Teasdale in this moment. Not just adamant but also amused she stands, in her fur collar and fur forearm warmers (or high cuffs?) and black gloves and fur muff and black hat and simple but indubitably genuine pearls—she is something. And does she look credulous? Does she look like a pushover? No. She is skeptical. She is confident in her skepticism. Her eyes flash. She smiles to herself.

If this woman's faith in Rufus T. Firefly is implicit, why shouldn't ours be?

You see how straightforwardly the *Freedonia Gazette* reports his accession: big banner headline (the visual news medium in 1933):

FIREFLY APPOINTED NEW LEADER OF FREEDONIA

And we pan down to a big photo of the man. So his mustache and eyebrows are smudges of greasepaint. (Originally, in vaudeville, Groucho glued on a more naturalistic version, but one night he was running late and greasepaint worked. For the movies, he was told, he would have to resort to something more convincing. Oh no, I won't, he said, and he was right. For TV, many years later, he would grow a real one. That's TV for you—rather than selling an imaginary mustache, it co-opts reality.)

Even if he didn't have the Teasdale endorsement, when we look in this man's eyes, are we going to question the credibility of someone who, on the very face of him, doesn't believe in anything?

Pan farther down to the subhead: we're going to have a "Mammoth Reception." And so we do.

Whew. Pretty fancy place here. Is it Mrs. Teasdale's home or the Freedonian reception palace? Either way, I am reminded of an anecdote in *Stranger at the Party*, a memoir by Helen Lawrenson. She's arriving at a party at the residence of Condé Nast (who at that time was a person):

> The private elevator leading to the penthouse at 1040 Park Avenue was loaded with Vanderbilts, Astors, Whitneys and their ilk, all dressed to kill, when two men squeezed in, just before the door closed. Once before, I had seen them without makeup, so I recognized them, but I doubt if the others did, because Groucho, minus fake eyebrows, mustache and spectacles, and Harpo, minus wig, looked ordinary to the point of anonymity. As we rode up, in dignified silence, the brothers looked us over and then Groucho said, loud and clear, "This is a classy joint." "Yeah," replied Harpo, just as loudly. "You said it!" The others acted as if they hadn't heard, eyes averted, while the two Marxes tried to keep from laughing.

"The Honorable Secretary of Finance and Parking" is introduced, with due fanfare, and His Excellency Ambassador Trentino of Sylvania: Louis Calhern, every inch the crooked statesman. More gravitas. Trentino is the first person we've met who is as tall as Mrs. Teasdale. (Calhern will go on to portray the distinguished American jurist Oliver William Holmes Jr. in *The Magnificent Yankee* and Julius Caesar to Marlon Brando's Mark Antony.) And Miss Vera Marcal, and the Honorable Pandu of Muftan . . .

Back up. At the risk of being borderline crass, let us get a load of Miss Vera Marcal. She is played by the Mexican-born Raquel Torres, age twenty-three, who earlier in 1933 appeared as "Leader of Amazon Women" (or "a passionate female Tarzan," according to some lucky duck on imdb.com who apparently has actually seen the movie) in something called *So This Is Africa*.

For all the romance in most of Leo McCarey's movies, there is no heavy breathing. I hope you have taken up my suggestion to check out, on YouTube, Leila Hyams's drum-instruction scene (ditta-boom) with Roland Young in *Ruggles of Red Gap*. That to me is romance of a high, unmushy order. Two people, clearly but not blatantly attracted to each other, getting playfully and respectfully acquainted. That scene was improvised. We may well imagine that McCarey, musing at the piano, said, "Leila, why don't you sit here, and Roland at the drums, and see what happens." There's another moment in *Ruggles* that grabs my heart. Charles Laughton is Ruggles, a valet whose employer loses him in a poker game to an amiable, rough-hewn character from Red Gap, Washington. So Ruggles must move to that place. The regular people there welcome him as an equal. The pretentious social set gets the notion, from his accent and manners, that he is nobility, so they fawn on him. A widow played by Zasu Pitts likes him for himself, but sort of assumes he is too aristocratic for her. Then there is a moment.

Neither Charles Laughton nor Zasu Pitts is a looker. She has a squeaky voice, and at one point in the filming McCarey said to

Laughton, "*Jesus,* Charles, do you *have* to be so nancy?" and Laughton replied, "But, my dear fellow, after eight o'clock a bit of it is *bound* to show." But they make an appealing potential couple. And the moment comes when his true station is revealed. "Oh, so you're not—" she says, brightening, and the way he springs toward her, happy to be recognized as no more aristocratic than she . . . I guess you have to see it.

Romance in McCarey's movies is all the more convincing for being cool. Miss Vera Marcal is hot. She is not only the sexiest woman in any Marx Brothers movie, including Thelma Todd in *Horse Feathers* (Chico gives her what I believe to be the only Marx Brother onscreen kiss,* a little ad-lib-looking peck after tickling the keys for her) and *Monkey Business,* and even Marilyn Monroe in the last-gasp, deeply unfortunate *Love Happy* (1949), she is also the sexiest woman in a Leo McCarey movie. (Ingrid Bergman, after all, plays a nun.) And see how Miss Vera Marcal is responded to! Poised as a temptress and fully qualified, she is appreciated by only one character.

Zeppo. Oh, Trentino kisses her hand and says he has seen her many times in the theater—and he is in cahoots with her. She is quite willing, for whatever reason, to help him bring Freedonia under Sylvanian control. (Which "may not be so ee-see," she says—little does she know.) She may well be his lover. In the Kalmar-Ruby script, she is referred to as his niece, a term with a certain euphemistic force in that day. But Trentino gives no sign

---

* In Ruby and Kalmar's largely abandoned *Duck Soup* script, Chico tells a prospective female spy that she will have to "make love to men. Come on—let's see you make love." So she "bends him over and kisses him madly," after which he "staggers around in a daze." No. That is not Chico. We don't want to see that.

of desiring anything but power. As he strokes Miss Vera's poufy pompon, or whatever it is, and tells her he is going to "place [Firefly] in your hands," *his* hand is within an inch of her profoundly palpable-looking cleavage. But the gleam in his eye is his plan to win Freedonia by wooing Mrs. Teasdale. Louis Calhern as Trentino evinces no more feeling for Miss Vera here than he will later for Ingrid Bergman in *Notorious*.

Doesn't faze Miss Vera. She's a go-along girl. But look at the way Zeppo looks at her. Unlike his brothers, Zeppo was conventionally handsome, almost. But not really. Most people's noses project. His nose line continued the slope of his forehead. If Bob Hope had a ski-jump nose, Zeppo's was straight downhill. And his eyes, though they were closer together than his brothers'—closer than most people's—had a certain freshness in them. Both of those eyes linger on Vera Marcal as he is introduced to her and he says, "We've met," and she says, "Of course." (Where have they met? In an earlier version of the script, Vera Marcal seduces Zeppo's character. McCarey cut that part out.)

That's about it for their relationship in *Duck Soup*, but there's something unnaturally natural going on with Zeppo. He has feelings for Vera that aren't prepubescent. His big brothers here (all in their forties) are four-year-olds. He is acting fourteen. If all the brothers went gaga over Vera, this would be a different story.

Here's an indelicate anecdote. In *Bring in the Peacocks: Memoirs of a Hollywood Producer*, Hank Moonjean tells of a celebrity-filled party in the fifties at the home of Burns and Allen. "Several people were gathered around Groucho Marx, who was holding court. The subject of Desilu Studios came up and how successful it had been for Lucille Ball and Desi Arnaz." Moonjean, as it happened, was a

good friend of Lucy's. "I asked Groucho how it was working with Lucy. Groucho said, without batting an eyelash, 'It was Zeppo who fucked her.'"

Groucho, please! Talk about iconoclasm! This is *Lucy* you're bandying about, and at the height of American Lucy-philia. Maybe you didn't mean it in the sexual sense. When, after *Duck Soup*, Zeppo was getting started as an agent, he agreed to semi-represent Lucy. If she heard of a part coming up that would be good for her, she should let him know and he'd see what he could do for her. Eventually Lucy concluded that when she told Zeppo about those parts, he got them for other actresses. (Of the Marxes, Lucy liked Harpo. At a dinner party he kindly explained how to eat the artichoke she had been on the verge of attacking with knife and fork. There's a scene for you. For a Leo McCarey movie. In a Marx Brothers movie, Harpo would not have been kind. And it would have been a pumpkin.)

Z eppo's character in *Duck Soup* is Bob Roland. He can't even catch a funny name. In Kalmar and Ruby's original treatment (entitled *Firecrackers,* later *Cracked Ice*), he was to play Bob Firestone. (Whoever changed Firestone to Firefly deserved to feel pretty good about it.) Bob's in love with Mrs. Teasdale's daughter, June, who is being pursued by the Trentino character (whose name at that stage was Frankenstein). Zeppo's end of this romance is pretty sappy. He's not even very intense about June: at one point

OPPOSITE: *Zeppo's seduction by Miss Vera Marcal was cut— no wonder he left the act.*

he professes his patriotic willingness to give her up for the sake of Freedonia, but she refuses to be given up. His original backstory relationship with Vera Marcal, whatever it may have been, is lost.

Note that Zeppo is still beaming at Vera as he breaks into song about the punctuality of Firefly. "The Clock on the Wall Strikes Ten." Thus is a note of momentousness sounded. The musical numbers that commence at this point are operetta-esque, evocative of Gilbert (Jewish) and Sullivan (Irish). Groucho was a big Gilbert and Sullivan fan, knew many of their songs by heart, and sang them obsessively. At the age of seventy, he was delighted to play Ko-Ko, the Lord High Executioner, in *The Mikado* on TV. (The critical consensus: more Groucho in kimono than Ko-Ko in *Mikado*.)

Okay, cue the clock. On the wall. Strikes ten. And here come the trumpeters, and the be-shako'ed swordsmen, and the toe dancers, scattering petals in the new leader's expected path, and the soldiers draw their swords to form an arch over the petals, and the dancers are down on their knees and extending their arms toward the new leader's expected entrance, and the distinguished guests bow in that same direction, and Freedonia, land of the brave and free, is hailed.

And hailed again.

And one more time.

Thus is the note of momentousness sustained, in the face of a creeping note of desperation. (In 2009 in England, a toddler who had been in a coma and was about to be taken off life support suddenly woke up singing the ABBA song "Mamma Mia." If I ever snap out of a coma singing something, I trust it will be "Hail, Hail, Freedonia, laaand of the braaaave and freeeee.")

Firefly strewing petals for himself was cut. Groucho is said to have freaked out the closest ballerina.

And Groucho slides down a pole to arrive at everyone's rear. All this is pretty much from Kalmar and Ruby's original treatment. In the eventual shooting script, Firefly was to direct the line, "You expecting somebody?" to one of the ballerinas. But, it is said, Groucho delivered the line so lecherously that she cried out, "No!"

If so, that would have been Firefly's only lecherous moment in this movie. As it is, he directs the question to one of the troopers, who answers yes, and Groucho falls into place beside him, holding his cigar up in line with the swords. He is awaiting himself.

This—by no means the movie's only Identity Issue moment—is

as good a place as any for another indelicate anecdote from Groucho's real life.

Over the years Harry Ruby was probably Groucho's best friend. Garson Kanin (who heard it from Ruby) writes that Ruby came to Groucho once for erotic assistance. Owing to a mix-up, Ruby had arranged for not one but two agreeable women to meet him at the Beverly Hills bungalow he maintained for such appointments. For Ruby, like Firefly, a gal a day was all he could handle. He wanted Groucho to make it a foursome.

No, said Groucho. He was fifty-nine, and he had given up "that foolishness." He didn't have it in him anymore.

Don't worry, said Ruby, he had a doctor who gave him regular shots that enabled him to "function." He'd take Groucho to that doctor right away.

Groucho still resisted, but Ruby kept pressing. Finally, he got Groucho as far as the Wilshire Medical Building. Groucho still resisted. Ruby had him by the arm and dragged him inside to the elevator. There they were joined by newborns, old people in wheelchairs, and someone shaking with tremors.

"Floors, please," said the elevator operator. "Speak up."

Groucho spoke up. He shouted:

"I can't get a hard-on! What floor is that?"

To me, two things stand out, so to speak, about that anecdote.

In the first place, fifty-nine is way too young. Don't tell me that Harpo or Chico or Zeppo were willing to give up on functioning at fifty-nine. By that age, Harpo, after a long adventurous bachelorhood, was joyfully married for life. Chico's compulsive womanizing had finally caused his wife to throw him out of the house, her heart broken ("After nineteen years of marriage," she had told their daughter, "if I hear his footstep, my heart races"), and all indications were that he still had it going on. Zeppo got married at fifty-eight and stayed married until he was seventy-one, to the future wife of Frank Sinatra. Not that the following is by any means proof of potency, but Zeppo was sued by a reputed mobster's estranged wife for roughing her up when he was seventy-seven. (And when he died, at seventy-eight, he left an automobile and a Safeway franchise to each of two women who were neither of his ex-wives.) At fifty-nine, Groucho was undoubtedly bummed by the recent failure of his second marriage, but still.

In the second place—talk about iconoclasm. I have known personally any number of men, and have read of many others, who were quick to put down sacred cows. Groucho is the only man I have ever heard of who, when presented with an opportunity—however apropos—to dismiss his own erectile capacity in a crowded elevator, before he was *sixty* even . . . Any other man, I'm saying, would have let that opportunity pass. While chuckling ruefully to himself maybe. When it comes to self-deprecation, most people would be satisfied with Groucho's famous remark that he wouldn't belong to any club that would accept him. But not Groucho, who wouldn't have been caught dead giving the impression that he had any joie de vivre. Here was a peerless leader indeed, who combined self-absorption and detachment from himself in a way that was genuinely radical. This is another of *Duck Soup*'s sources of authority.

If Groucho arrived carrying a sword, or any conventionally empowering scepter, we would think less of him. He has the balls to carry that cigar. Sometimes, as Freud is supposed to have said, a cigar is only a cigar. For the Marx Brothers, it is a prop. See the insanely prolonged scene in *At the Circus* in which Chico keeps coming up with another one to give the strongman, when the point was to get the strongman to bring out one of *his* cigars because, for reasons unnecessary to go into here, it is needed as evidence. And see the scene coming up in *Duck Soup* in which Harpo and Chico play baseball with a cigar. As it happens, a major league pitcher, George Culver of the Cincinnati Reds, told me years ago that he gave up smoking because it detracted from the circulation in his fingertips and therefore from his feel for the ball. Conceivably, cigar smoking numbed Groucho's member (see "wouldn't belong to any club" above) in that unfortunate way. However that may be, it is clear that his johnson played second fiddle to his wisecrack jones.

On the set of *A Day at the Races*, in 1937, Groucho had a crush on the female love interest, Maureen O'Sullivan. After his death, she reminisced that he was "very sexy. He had physical presence and a good build." But when he took her to lunch, he wouldn't quit with the jokes. "Groucho never knew how to talk normally," she said. "His life was his jokes." Graham Greene, in his review of *A Day at the Races*, wrote that he was quite taken by this winsome colleen himself, but "Miss O'Sullivan is a real person," and therefore had no business in the Marxes' world, for "real people do more than retard, they smash the Marx fantasy. When Groucho lopes into the inane, they smile at him incredulously (being real people they cannot take him for granted), and there was one dreadful moment when Miss O'Sullivan murmured the word 'Silly.' Silly—good God, we cannot help exclaiming since we are real people too, have we been deceived all along?"

Anyway, O'Sullivan was trying to keep her marriage to John Farrow together. This is the marriage that produced Mia Farrow.

I'm way ahead of you. You're thinking that if Groucho had taken O'Sullivan away, he could have become not only Woody Allen's idol but his stepfather-in-law. But no. Mia Farrow was not born until eight years after the filming of *A Day at the Races*. All we can say about what would have happened if Groucho and Maureen O'Sullivan had had a daughter is that Groucho, given his track record with daughters, would have doted upon and then alienated her.

Let us pause for a moment to applaud the absence of real people in *Duck Soup*.

O n noticing that the guest of honor has materialized from opposite the expected direction, Mrs. Teasdale welcomes him "with open arms." We cut to a two-shot (in which, continuity nuts may notice, Firefly's swallowtail coat has become a jacket of a lighter shade with black piping and a glove in the breast pocket). I will not quote all of the resultant dialogue here. Groucho once expressed resentment of authors who "do a new kind of writing. They rent our movies . . . and write down all the good jokes in their books. Quite a writing feat!" Suffice it to say that Firefly responds to the opening provided by his gracious hostess by accusing her of coming on to him, of being comparable to a large building (she is in fact quite a bit taller than he), and of murdering her husband. He tells her to leave the premises. Then he ascertains that she is very rich and says, "Can't you see what I'm trying to tell you? I love you."

This dialogue is not characteristic of McCarey. It was presumably laid down by layer upon layer of Kalmar, Ruby, Sheekman,

Perrin, Mankiewicz, and Marx. I'd say its non-sequitur zippiness derives to some extent from the pre-talking-picture humor-writing tradition of Benchley, Ring Lardner (check out his nonsense plays and lines in his stories like " 'Shut up,' he explained"), and S. J. Perelman, who helped write *Monkey Business* and *Horse Feathers*. But such alchemical progressions as these did not manifest themselves through anyone in American culture but Groucho. It is fine, bughouse stuff, and it leaves the widder Teasdale blushing with delight at his declaration of love. Then we get what is for my money a particularly inspired exchange (it comes straight from the Ruby-Kalmar treatment, but from much later in the plot):

"Oh, Your Excellency!"

"You're not so bad yourself," he says, rolling his eyes in mock-modest gratification.

At this point let us address an enduring question: the extent to which Margaret Dumont, this pillar of Marx Brothers comedy, appreciated the humor in any of it. Groucho always maintained that she didn't get any of the jokes, didn't even realize they were jokes. Maureen O'Sullivan said that Dumont told her, when shooting of *A Day at the Races* was about to begin, "It's not going to be one of *those* things. I'm having a very *serious* part this time." In fact, she is much sillier in that movie than in *Duck Soup*. At one point she remarks that Groucho's character (a veterinarian) "tells me I'm the only case in history: I have high blood pressure on my right side and low blood pressure on my left side." And she must have been aware of how silly it was.

Who was Margaret Dumont? From the book *Hello, I Must Be Going* by Charlotte Chandler, I got the impression that she grew up in Atlanta in the home of her godfather, Joel Chandler Harris, author of the Uncle Remus stories. Even though a descendant of Harris assured me that this wasn't true, I want to believe it, in part because I grew up in that area myself, in part because Harris adds another Irish-American element to the whole tapestry here, and in part because I like to imagine B'rer Rabbit and Margaret Dumont doing a scene together. Last time I looked, both the International Movie Data Base (the indispensable imdb.com) and a blog on the website of the Wren's Nest, the preserved home of Joel Chandler Harris, were still putting Dumont forward as Harris's goddaughter. And my researches turned up a young woman relative, Essie LaRose, who came to live in the Harris household. Essie was conceivably about the right age if Ms. Dumont had not been quite truthful about hers, and a photo of her resembled an early one of Ms. Dumont.

But no. Essie married a man named Kelly, had children, and lived out her life in Atlanta. In his biography of the Marx Brothers, *Monkey Business,* Simon Louvish establishes that Margaret Dumont was born Daisy Baker in Brooklyn, New York, in 1882 (so she was only six years younger than Essie). Her father was an Irish seaman, her mother a French vocalist. Daisy became a showgirl. In 1915 she married an heir to a sugar fortune. In 1918 he died. She was presumably not left as well off as Mrs. Teasdale because she went right back to work—changing her birth date to 1889 and her name (*marguerite,* Louvish points out, is French for "daisy") to something more aristocratic.

George S. Kaufman, who found Dumont for the Marxes, wrote of her in his autobiography:

I strongly suspect that she was convinced that great ladies weren't expected to have great intellects, and she responded accordingly . . . No one could have been a showgirl for as many years as she was without acquiring at least a modicum of street savvy. If my theory is correct, then she should be lauded for the longest running performance in show business history, for she never slipped from her character until her death.

In 1972 Groucho's controversial young late-life companion, Erin Fleming, interviewed him for *Vogue*. "You never use the word 'lady,'" she observed.

"You're damn right," he replied. "I hate that word. What is a 'lady' supposed to be anyway? Some broad with white gloves on that you can't even approach?"

Let us stipulate right away that Groucho in real life was no boon to women. Zeppo said Groucho tended to go for women who weren't very smart and then to make cruel fun of them for not being very smart. But Groucho, and American culture in general, had reason to resist the concept of *lady,* especially with white gloves on. Marcia Davenport, novelist and daughter of the classical vocalist Alma Gluck, wrote in her memoir, *Too Strong for Fantasy,* of taking her mother to see *The Cocoanuts* on stage in Philadelphia:

> In the lobby amongst the incoming crowd were several of my grande dame friends who were plainly very pleased to meet my mother. Some of them sat in the row behind us and we chatted until the show began. It was a riot—and Philadelphia sat on its hands. We were fuming. The boys

worked hard. The audience was a dud. Groucho in desperation came down to the footlights and began a wild, zany soliloquy which elsewhere would have had the audience howling. Nothing here. He scanned the house, looking for something, anything, to which he could pin a gag. Suddenly his face lit up, he went down on one knee like Al Jolson, arms outstretched, and shouted, "*Oy!* Alma Gluck!"

We could feel the freeze from the ladies behind us.

After Dumont announced her retirement, Chico's daughter, Maxine, who remembered her fondly, called her up, and they met for lunch. (You can get a sense of Chico's charm from the fact that his daughter seems to be the sort of person who remembers everyone fondly. She says "Uncle Groucho" gave her "unconditional love.") Dumont showed up in long gloves and with a lorgnette. "The boys," she said in that voice, "ruined my career." Nobody would take her seriously as an actress. "People always thought they saw Groucho peering from behind my skirt."

As proof that Dumont was not in on the jokes,* Groucho often

---

* When Bob Roland (Zeppo) tells Firefly that Trentino slapped Bob when he told an off-color story to Vera Marcal, and Firefly wants to know what the story was, and Bob whispers it to him, and Firefly slaps him and demands to know where he heard such a story, and Bob says, "Well, you told it to me," and Firefly says, "Oh yes"—so far, so good, but it seems odd for him to claim then that he heard it from Mrs. Teasdale. In real life, Groucho didn't care much for jokes as such, but he did like to tell one of Chico's favorites. It seems a man got lost in the woods for days, and he was hungry and thirsty, but what was driving him mad was having no female companionship. So when he came to a cabin, the first thing that caught his eye was a knothole. Something about it was so inviting that he couldn't help himself, he pulled down his pants and inserted his member into the hole and was pounding away when a man came to the door and said, "Excuse me, but could you come inside, and do that toward the outside? We're just sitting down to dinner."

cited her reaction to a line in the *Duck Soup* finale: "We're alone in a small cottage and there's a war going on outside and Margaret says to me, 'What are you doing, Rufus?' And I say, 'I'm fighting for your honor, which is probably more than you ever did.' Later she asked me what I meant by that."

It's neither a foolish nor necessarily a humorless question. When Dumont was out of work, Groucho tried to get friends to hire her—stressing, in his letters to them, her need and abject availability rather than her talent. Two weeks before she died of a stroke in 1965, at eighty-three, she appeared as a special guest on the television variety show *Hollywood Palace*, hosted that week by Groucho. They did the "Hurray for Captain Spaulding" number. "After the show," Groucho recalled, "she stood by the stage door with a bouquet of roses, which she probably sent herself. She was waiting to be picked up. A few minutes later some guy came along in a crummy car and took her away. She was always a lady, a wonderful person. Died without any money."

Among the young people dancing attendance on Groucho in the *Hollywood Palace* number (see YouTube), Dumont looks game but a little bit lost. Groucho says, "Sing it, Margie!" at one point, but he's not connecting. He steps on a couple of her lines while accusing her of stepping on his. Couldn't *he* have sent her some roses?

Back to Freedonia. Enter Trentino. Mrs. T introduces him to Firefly, who tries to borrow $20 million from him, okay, then, how about twelve dollars till payday, insults him, drives him away. Next introduction is to Vera Marcal. Firefly lurches right past her (a quick flash of his signature upper-body-forward walk, which caused Oscar

Levant to say, "I wouldn't stoop so high"),* looking for someone who answers, to his satisfaction, the description of "a very charming lady." Even when Mrs. T directs his attention to Vera, he hardly looks at her, but instead tries to impress her with dance moves. These moves are somewhat less supple and droll than the ones he shows off at a similar moment in *Animal Crackers,* but they are more than supple and droll enough for the stiffs at this reception.

---

* Groucho's walk contradicts itself: he slouches, and yet he scoots. Raymond Durgnat called it a "sneaky, bent-double walk-cum-slide," a "physical metaphor for moral snakeyness," and "a sleek hunchbacked lope." Stefan Kanfer: "that hilarious slinking crouch." Jack Kerouac: "that furious, ground-hugging walk with coattails flying." Max Eastman: Groucho "bends in the middle in a highly impractical manner, as though he were working himself not very successfully on a pair of ill-adjusted hinges." And yet the walk has a certain psychological universality. Groucho was indignant when George S. Kaufman's biographer suggested that the walk imitated the way Kaufman paced around while thinking, but the walk's thrust (unlike that of trucking, in which the head cools it in the wake of the strut) does seem cerebral. "Headstrong," Trentino will call Firefly, and in this walk there is something of a locomotive writing a check its caboose can't cash. Robert Benchley, according to his son Nathaniel, had "a slightly stooped forward, stern-out kind of walk that he used when intent on accomplishing something . . . as though he were already on the defensive against the inanimate objects that were about to lash out at him." Benchley's gait befit a lovable bumbler. Groucho's is exhilarating for the way his head expects the rest of him to look after itself. In 2003 researchers who had studied slow-motion film of elephants making haste reported that the animals did what could be described as "Groucho running"—a kind of headlong, bent-leg shuffle. (That's hard to see, though, even in slo-mo, when the elephants come running, as we shall see, to join Freedonia's war.) Groucho, for his part, said that in vaudeville "I was just kidding around one day and started to walk funny. The audience liked it so I left it in." When Harpo tries to alert Chico to something Groucho is doing in *A Day at the Races* by imitating the walk with his finger beneath his nose like a mustache, Chico's first guess is "Buffalo Bill goes ice skating." Now people teach others how to "Groucho walk," not for comedic purposes but as a dance move, as an exercise for butt and thigh muscles, as a handheld-camera-steadying technique, as a gun-steadying technique for target shooting or police work, or as the best way to approach a running helicopter safely. It may be (Michael Jackson's moonwalk being a contender) the best-known walk in history.

The "till-the-cows-come-home" joke with which he drives Vera away is more confusing than insulting, but Firefly doesn't care. He demands to know where his secretary is, and right on the beat there is Zeppo behind him, startling him into one of his patented, quick-as-a-hiccup, panicky scrambles. We think of Groucho as the verbal Marx, but within the range of his character he is as fine a physical comedian as Harpo.

The take-a-letter joke (in which some commentators have detected another Identity Issue), he's playing air-hopscotch as Mrs. T tells him the eyes of the world are upon him, and from there we swing into the admirably fluid intricacy of the next musical number. Groucho plays "Dixie" on a flute while holding on to his cigar. He conducts with a flourish or two the chorus of absurdly caparisoned guests of all nations, among whom he weaves himself with aplomb. And he lays out the goals of his administration. This being the land of the free, he will oppose exhibitions of pleasure (shades of Woody Allen's invocations of "anhedonia"), but primarily he will be corrupt. (There's a nice frown-to-smile-of-relief reaction from a bulky, white-haired man wearing a sash as Firefly first comes out against graft and then makes it clear that he means graft he doesn't get a taste of.) And he will be, avowedly, even more ruinous than his predecessor.

This sort of thing (let alone the forthcoming court scene, and the musical number that saved the Woody Allen character's life) would not have been exhibitable one year later, when the Hollywood Production Code—drafted by a Jesuit priest and a Catholic layman— began to be strictly enforced by the Irish-American Joseph Breen. The Code forbade moral relativism and disrespect for social order. So much for the Marx Brothers at their most intense.

In Freedonia in 1933, however, amorality goes down well. You'll notice the international crowd singing along heartily enough as Firefly winds up standing next to a footman in knee breeches, with his own pants up in solidarity. The Groucho walk was well suited to rolling up one's pants in motion.*

There is a limit to Mrs. T's tolerance: "Good heavens!"

May we pause just a moment to regret the loss to high comedy of expressions like "Good heavens!" and Trentino's forthcoming "Gentlemen, please!" Contemporary substitutes like "Holy shit!" and "Stop acting like such assholes!" lack elegance.

"You *cahn't* go" to meet with the House of Representatives (evidently a higher-toned one than the American one today) "with your *trous*ahs up!" Mrs. T exclaims in horror.

Any of us could have written Groucho's rejoinder. But who among us, with pants up or down, while singing "ah-a-a-a-ah," and then, still, while being reproached for disorderly attire, could look so fetchingly like a cynical baby bird?

Enter Harpo, finally, after twelve and a half minutes. Not my favorite Harpo entrance.† Pinky is his character's name, a change from Brownie and from Skippy. Note that he surreptitiously establishes himself as a spy by taking a snapshot of Firefly and scrawling some notes. When Firefly (back in the dark coat, with shirttail out) says, "Step on it," they do the driving-off-and-leaving-the-sidecar bit, which is from the original treatment.

This is one of the few bits in *Duck Soup* that would have been

---

* In midnote, he's got the gray jacket back on, but without the glove in the pocket. McCarey seems to have gone with the best takes rather than matching ones.
† Nowhere near as good as in *Animal Crackers,* when a butler announces him as "the Professor," and he saunters in wearing a long black cape and top hat and puffing a cigarette, and Groucho says, "The gate swung open and a fig newton entered."

hard to do, and probably ineffective, onstage. *Horse Feathers* has a canoe scene and a football game. *Duck Soup* is almost all indoors. Yet *Duck Soup* flows more cinematically than the previous Marx films. How did it get that way?

No one knows how many drafts there were of the Kalmar-Ruby script. At www.marx-brothers.org/marxology/, you can find a scanned copy of their original treatment, dated December 1932, with one of the tentative titles, "Firecrackers," crossed out and replaced by "Cracked Ice." You can also find online an expansion of that treatment in the form of the "Second Temporary Script" of "Cracked Ice," dated January 18, 1933, and credited to Kalmar and Ruby and also to one Grover Jones, a veteran journeyman screen-writer who had contributed to Lubitsch's great *Trouble in Paradise*, adapted from the stage, and in 1936 would do some work for McCarey on *The Milky Way*. This is the last we hear, in connection with *Duck Soup*, of Grover Jones.

There's something naked about a movie script. I have written a few of them, and every time I turned one of them in, the feeling came upon me that I had dug up one of those drawings of cool spaceships I did in grade school and presented it to NASA. Or that I had proposed to put into the mouth of a mother superior words of love that would never pass the lips of a common whore, or vice versa. At best, a great deal of reification remained to be done. S. J. Perelman has left us a chilling account of reading aloud the first draft of the script of *Monkey Business* to a roomful of Marxes and Marx-related persons whose reactions ranged from scowls to naps to derision. We don't know how the Kalmar-Ruby efforts were received, but we ourselves, having seen the movie, can wince when we read some of what they wrote: why in the world would anybody want *that* to be in *Duck Soup*? Part of me, literary chap that I am, would like to believe that filming corrupts a script, but I know that is wrong—certainly in this case. *Duck Soup* is a great deal more refined than "Cracked Ice."

McCarey brought the principals—presumably the brothers, Kalmar, Ruby, Mankiewicz, Perrin, and Sheekman—to his Malibu beach house for gag plotting and rehearsal. Groucho, Chico, Perrin, and Sheekman were just back from New York, where they had collaborated on a radio series, *Flywheel, Shyster, and Flywheel,* about an unscrupulous lawyer and his Chico-ic assistant. Fifteen bits and routines in *Duck Soup*—including the line "Go, and never darken my towels again," and Chicolini's account to Trentino of shadowing Firefly—were lifted directly from episodes of the radio show. We don't know what went on in that beach house.

We do know that the brothers had comedy in their bones. Kalmar and Ruby had a fine high facility for comic song. Mankiewicz and the gagmen were fonts of crazy patter. And McCarey knew how to set up low and high comedy for capture on film. *Duck Soup* derives energies and strategies from European busking (the brothers' maternal grandparents were on the road in Germany as ventriloquist and harpist), operetta, vaudeville, Broadway, silent films, written humor of the *New Yorker* school, network radio, and early talkies. Another 1933 comedy from Paramount, W. C. Fields in *International House,* comprises many of these elements, as well as others:

Barleycornism.

Cab Calloway and band rendering "that funny funny funny
'Reefer Man.'"

In the role of herself (Fields calls her "my little fuzzy wishwash"), Peggy Hopkins Joyce. She was a notorious glamour gal and gold digger whose favors Harpo thought he was about to enjoy one night, but she just wanted him to sprawl with her on a divan and read to her from comic books, which he did for hours, and then . . . she wanted him to read to her some more, this time from news clippings about herself. So he went home.

Exploitation of pre-Code leeway to the point of out-and-out anatomical jokes. Squeezed into the front seat of a car, Ms. Joyce keeps complaining that she is "sitting on something" ("I lost mine in the market," says Fields), which turns out to be a cat.

Franklin Pangborn, and all that he implies.

Furthermore, the McGuffin of *International House,* a "radio-scope," invented by the Doctor Wong character played by our own Edmund Breese, is . . . television. But this is a movie in which Rudy Vallee croons "Thank Heaven for You" *to,* as opposed to through, his megaphone. Baby Rose Marie stands on a piano singing "My Bluebird's Singing the Blues." *International House* is a hodgepodge, a gallimaufry, a fuzzy mishmash. *Duck Soup* is a seamless blend of just about every form of American comedy up to its time. Never had the whole history of American comedy been brought to such a head, and never would it be again.

Sylvania, ho! Looks quite a bit like Freedonia, only rockier maybe, and as to its rooftops, less pointy. Can't these two homey-looking countries live in peace? Certainly not.

Enter Leonid Kinskey, as the frustrated "Sylvanian agitator." Note the pamphlets stuffed into his pocket. He has not been able to start what Trentino calls "the revolution as planned." Pamphlets? Plans? What use are such bagatelles in this movie?

In real life, Kinskey was no Red, nor was he feckless. According to imdb.com, he was born in St. Petersburg, Russia, in 1903. After the revolution he left the homeland and traveled through Europe and Latin America, picking up acting jobs along the way, before reaching the United States and, in 1932, appearing as a bit-part radical in *Trouble in Paradise*. After *Duck Soup* he played a snake charmer in *Lives of a Bengal Lancer,* an Arab in *The Garden of Allah,* Pierre in *That Night in Rio,* Professor Quintana in *Ball of Fire,* and most notably Sascha, the engaging bartender, in *Casablanca.* When Rick enables the young couple to win at roulette so that they can pay for exit visas, Sascha kisses him on both cheeks and says, "You have done a beautiful thing!"

> **RICK:** Get outa here, you crazy Russian.

Kinskey took that part away from Leo Mostovoy, another Russian émigré, as a result of becoming Bogart's drinking buddy during filming. In *Rhythm on the Range,* he and Bing Crosby introduced the song "I'm an Old Cowhand (from the Rio Grande)." He could have had a steady TV gig in *Hogan's Heroes,* but after appearing in the pilot as one of the heroes in the World War II prison camp, he withdrew from the series, saying, "The premise to me was both false and offensive. The Nazis were seldom dumb and never funny." He did a lot of other TV work, and died at ninety-five in Arizona.

Harpo, by the way, went to Russia, alone, right after the filming of *Duck Soup*. His friend and fellow "ardent New Dealer," the preposterous but influential *New York Times* drama critic Alexander Woollcott, had arranged the trip as a venture in cultural exchange: how could a Marx not be embraced by the Communists? On the way to Russia, Harpo had "planned to sort of mosey through Germany and see the sights. I did not mosey, however."

Hitler had been in power for six months. *Duck Soup*, said Harpo, was his most difficult movie, and the only one in which he worried about his performance. Not because of the director or the script. "The trouble was Adolph Hitler." American radio was broadcasting Hitler's speeches, and "twice we suspended shooting to listen to him scream."

In Hamburg, Harpo "saw the most frightening, most depressing sight I had ever seen—a row of stores with Stars of David and the word *Jude* painted on them, and inside, behind half-empty counters, people in a daze, cringing like they didn't know what hit them and didn't know where the next blow was coming from." But then, Harpo was no great thinker. At about this same time the greatest philosopher of the age, Martin Heidegger, was reacting differently to the rise of Fascism: he joined the Nazi Party, became rector of Freiberg University, and saw to it that all Jewish professors were sacked.

Russia was also intimidating, but eventually Harpo wowed Russian audiences with evenings of shtick; when Foreign Minister

Maxim Litvinov came onstage one night and shook hands with Harpo, a stream of silverware poured from Litvinov's sleeve. This was an old trick of Harpo's, the point being that Harpo's character had stolen everything he could get ahold of in some fancy mansion to which he had unaccountably been invited, so it is hard to say exactly why it played so well when Stalin's number two pulled it in 1933 Moscow, but it did—it killed.

Karl Marx, it must be said, had more in common with Harpo, or McCarey, than with the hangdog provocateur played by Kinskey in *Duck Soup*. According to Francis Wheen's biography of him, Marx and his friends Edgar Bauer and Wilhelm Liebknecht once, after having a number of beers in a series of London pubs, accosted a group of quiet diners and informed them that "snobbish, cant-ridden England was fit only for philistines." And then ran, and started breaking streetlamps by throwing paving stones. They attracted the attention of police. "Marx," recalled Liebknecht, "showed an agility I should not have attributed to him." The three made several quick turns and came up *behind* the police who were pursuing them.

Edmund Wilson called Marx "the greatest ironist since Swift." As a student, Marx wrote verse mocking Hegel's opaqueness:

He understands what he thinks, freely invents what he feels.
Thus, each may for himself suck wisdom's nourishing
    nectar;
Now you know all, since I've said plenty of nothing to you!

If I knew more about Marxism, I might make an argument that the brothers in *Duck Soup* are a kind of flip-side Karl, seizing the means of counterproduction in order to make money. I don't know

much about capitalism either, but I'll say this: the Marxes' fine abandon diminished as Hollywood figured out how to capitalize on them financially. They played it safer, and their movies, at least after *A Night at the Opera,* became more lucrative and less free.

Where were we? Trentino's office. Kinskey's agitator says he has failed to foment because Firefly is so popular with the people. Trentino, rather than expressing consternation, says (one of my favorite lines, somehow, in the whole movie), "Oh yes, I've known of that too."

So he has employed spies. Chicolini and Pinky. Chico and Harpo.

In childhood, Chico and Harpo were close, but not equal. Harpo: "I was flattered when people said I was the image of Chico. I guess I was. We were both of us shrimps compared to the average galoots in the neighborhood. We were skinny, with peaked faces, big eyes, and mops of wavy, unruly hair." But although "I practiced walking like Chico for hours," Harpo "never could master his look of total concentration."

Anything Harpo acquired that was spendable or hockable, Chico would steal. He even stole Harpo's bar mitzvah watch and, when Harpo complained, handed him the pawn ticket. Minnie bailed the watch out. Harpo prevented Chico from pawning it again by taking the hands off it—it still ticked just fine. But Chico also taught Harpo things: for instance, never shoot dice on a blanket.

As Harpo comes in backward with whirling eyes on the back of his head, Chico as Chicolini makes his first appearance. He's smiling. We can see confirmation here, without dwelling on it, of what so many people said who knew Chico in person: that he had a powerfully seductive smile. Not gigolo seductive, not salesman seduc-

tive, but deep-tissue seductive. It's not *warm,* it's not *confiding,* it's a got-something-working smile. It's a smile you'd like to respond to in such a way as to make it warmer. The thing that my wife likes most about the Marx Brothers is watching Chico play the piano. Which he doesn't do in this movie. A pity.

Why is it that Trentino welcomes his spies with what seems to be genuine enthusiasm? *"Gentlemen!"*

They run right past him and start messing with stuff on his desk. "Gentlemen! What is this?"

"Shhh. This is spy stuff." Richard Nixon once recorded himself saying, "The Jews are born spies." Anyone taking that contention seriously enough to refute it might point to this movie. One thing

Chicolini, Trentino, and Pinky: this is spy stuff.

to say for Harpo as a spy, he is resourceful: if you can't light your cigar with a telephone, the blowtorch you're carrying in your pants (same pocket you carry your alarm clock in) will do. After you light the cigar of the man you are reporting to, it's textbook spy-craft to cut it in half with the scissors you are carrying in that same pocket. Where is your James Bond when Harpo and Chico take up spying? Bond needed enemies to bring out his heroics; these spies foil whoever is handy.

Speaking of handy, why doesn't Harpo chase the secretary? He is about to, but when Chico says, "Anh-anh," he backs off. As a rule, Harpo does exactly what he wants to—when he takes scissors to his employer's coattails or applies glue to the seat of his employer's pants, he achieves that rare thing, an intended consequence. But Harpo does not pursue the secretary. No time for lust. Three-hundred-and-sixty-degree treason is a far far finer thing that they do.*

"Gentlemen, we are not getting anywhere!"

To that appeal, the spies' lightning response is unexpected: an improvised spot of baseball, with ruler for bat and cigar butt for ball. The Marxes were sports guys. In golf, Groucho once got a hole in one; Harpo says he missed a hole in one by inches, on another occasion, while not wearing any clothes. They were serious fans of baseball—Harpo a heavy-betting one. Harpo's boyhood dream was to play left field for the New York Giants because the left fielder was the only player he could see when he watched the games at the Polo Grounds for free from a promontory overlooking the park. In a celebrity baseball game, Will Rogers, playing second base, took a

---

* Far be it from me to indulge in loose speculation, but the secretary is played by Verna Hillie, age nineteen, who would go on to a small role in McCarey's next picture, *Six of a Kind*. Maybe McCarey chased her.

throw standing several feet from the bag and declared that Groucho, steaming into second, was out. "You've got to touch the base!" insisted Groucho. "When you're my age," said Rogers, "the base is wherever I'm standing." For Harpo and Chico, wherever they are is off-base, and home.

Freeze the frame right after they depart Trentino's office. Look closely at the copy of the *Freedonia Gazette* that, thanks to Harpo, is glued to Trentino's pants. It's the same copy that Trentino was holding up when he was finding fault with the agitator. Its banner headline is "Reception Tomorrow for Rufus T. Firefly." The last *Gazette* we saw said: "Mammoth Reception Arranged to Welcome Nation's Leader Tonight," and then we saw the reception. So Trentino is the type of national leader who reads old out-of-town newspapers. That still does not account for his parting words to Pinky and Chicolini: "Gentlemen, I'm going to give you one more chance." As Joe Adamson puts it in *Groucho, Harpo, Chico, and Sometimes Zeppo:*

> One more *chance*? What does he *want*? What are his prerequisites for despondency? Leprosy? The Black Plague? Fire, Famine and Slaughter? Apparently games and disguises are all that's expected of a spy anymore . . .

In Kalmar and Ruby's original treatment, the spy stuff is different. Groucho and Chico are interviewing young women, ostensibly to hire one as a spy, but mostly so they can ogle them and get their phone numbers. Then Harpo enters the waiting room, in drag, and squeezes in between two girls. He's carrying a "very large pocket book," from which he extracts an outsize powder puff, with which he suffuses the room in powder. When one of the girls tells a dumb joke, Harpo slaps her on the leg, she slaps him, he slaps her again on the leg, and she looks at her leg and it's bruised from the slap.

We don't want to see that, do we? No. Kalmar and Ruby's treatment and the draft of their subsequent script that survives contain many of the movie's best bits, but they also include stuff that was too crass and prurient to get past McCarey. For instance, Kalmar and Ruby have Harpo in female garb entering the interview room, where he is well received. Chico advises him that if he gets the job of woman spy, he "might have to make love." Harpo expresses his delight at that prospect by hugging Chico, who hugs back. There's a pop—Harpo's right breast has gone flat. Harpo finds a pump somewhere on his person and manages to explode his other breast. When he tries to pump that up, instead his butt expands, to the point that his dress comes off and he's in his "trunks."

"Well, you fooled me," says Chico, in the script, so Harpo is hired. They give him a spyglass, which he trains out a window to find "a beautiful girl across the way getting undressed for bed." He hands the spyglass to Groucho and Chico, who are impressed by this bit of spycraft, but then who should pop up in the view but Harpo chasing the girl around the room and then outside.

Enough of the script—back to the movie. We find Groucho in Freedonia playing jacks, and showing pride in his jacks-playing skill, as his distinguished-looking cabinet ministers wait to be called to order. Then there's his still-oft-quoted "run out and find me a four-year-old child" joke. And he dispenses with new business and old. Imdb.com says that Edward Arnold plays one of the politicians in *Duck Soup*, but I've never been able to find him. Might he have been confused with Edwin Maxwell, who looks quite a bit like Arnold? Maxwell, uncredited, is the Secretary of War, who resigns in this scene. In 1933 Maxwell appeared in twenty-one movies, including his fairly substantial and quite creepy role in *Mystery of the Wax Museum*, which you might want to check out sometime.

But never mind that. By the equivalent point in Kalmar and Ruby's script, it has been established that Firefly is an arms dealer. *That's* why he's trying to stir up war with Sylvania—so he can sell arms. So explicable, so mundane. In the movie, he's just naturally interested in havoc. And so are his brothers.

In Kalmar and Ruby's script, Firefly is in his House of Representatives, with Trentino visiting. We hear Chico chanting "PEANUTS" outside. Firefly tells Trentino to scram, then tells Zeppo to chase the vendor away. Zeppo says he won't go, so Groucho goes to the window and sees Chico at his peanut stand conniving with Trentino, who, we learn, has hired Chico and Harpo to drive Firefly crazy. *What?* It's so much more fun to drive Trentino crazy.

But here's who would be even more fun to drive crazy: a beefy Irishman. Irish kids weren't the only bullies Harpo recalled in *Harpo Speaks!* As Harpo broke it down, a German kid whose father had licked him for street fighting would take it out on an Italian kid who would pass it on to an Irish kid who would avenge himself on a Jewish kid, and at every stage the message was "I'll teach you!"—something Harpo always thought of, he said, when anyone mentioned "progressive education."

Chico finessed the diversity problem by mastering Irish, Italian, and German accents so that he could pass himself off as ethnically appropriate on any block. But Harpo's talents were not vocal, and at any rate there was no fooling the Irish who knew him. He dropped out of school in the second grade, Harpo recalled, for two reasons:

> One was a big Irish kid in my class and the other was a
> bigger Irish kid. I was a perfect patsy for them, a marked
> victim. I was small for my age. I had a high, squeaky voice.
> And I was the only Jewish boy in the room.

Whenever the teacher left the room, the Irish boys, according to Harpo, would throw him out the window. One day he just stayed out, for good.

We know that Harpo, as a performer, was McCarey's favorite Marx brother. Maybe it didn't occur to McCarey that giving Harpo a large Irishman to push around would be sweet. Maybe McCarey thought having a large Irishman to push around would keep the Marxes from trying to push him around. At any rate, McCarey brought in Edgar Kennedy, whom he'd worked with in the Laurel and Hardy days, to play a lemonade seller.

McCarey and Kennedy were old masters of the slow burn and the tit-for-tat. One of McCarey's contributions to silent comedy had been to slow down the pace. For one thing, he shot at a speed of fifteen or sixteen frames per second, instead of the previously standard twelve, so that gags weren't jerky and frenetic. For another thing, he got his actors to pause more, to engage in deliberative slapstick. This would give them time to fume, to steam, to plot and scheme, and for the audience to savor the last bit and to anticipate the next bit of tit-for-tat. In an interview with *Cahiers du Cinéma*, McCarey recalled a scene in one of his Laurel and Hardy shorts, *From Soup to Nuts*: Hardy, carrying a cake, steps through a doorway and

> falls and finds himself on the floor, his head buried in the
> cake. I shouted to him, "Don't move! Above all, don't move!

Stay like that, the cake should burn your face!" And for a minute and a half, the public couldn't stop laughing. Hardy remained immobile, his head in the cake! He remained stretched out, furious, and you could only see his back.

McCarey's devotion to the tit-for-tat derived, he maintained, from a party he attended in the twenties with Hal Roach, Charley Chase, Mabel Normand, and other giants of the silent screen. He had never been able to tie a bow tie. Normand had promised to tie his black tie for him at his hotel, but as a joke she ducked out, so he had to call all around to track down a friend's wife whom he knew to be an excellent tier of ties. Then as soon as he got to the party, Normand pulled the tie loose. So McCarey pulled Roach's. Roach pulled somebody else's. Soon everyone at the affair was ripping off collars and tearing apart dinner jackets. That social occasion, McCarey recalled, inspired "at least a dozen Laurel and Hardy pictures."

The next scene of *Duck Soup* is in the tradition of tit-for-tat, but it's different, because it's the Marxes. In Laurel and Hardy movies, tit-for-tat was a matter of carrying out mutual assured destruction. When Harpo and Chico get ahold of Edgar Kennedy, it's more like tit-tit-tit-tit-tit for the Marxes, Kennedy getting in one resounding tat, and then more tits for the Marxes. Kennedy can't keep up because he is operating at a slow-burn pace and they are operating at pretty close to their usual rat-a-tat.

So that you don't have to, I have watched this scene some twenty or thirty times, and in slow motion, and frame by frame. A lot of things happen, and here they are, for the record:

Chico, at his peanut wagon, is chanting, "PEA-NUTS," but his focus, and his big anticipatory smile, is on the wiener he is mustarding up. Harpo appears. Steals some peanuts. That makes sense. But it is not enough for Harpo. Harpo pulls out his scissors and snips Chico's wiener in two.

Why? In a Laurel and Hardy movie, a tit-for-tat would be generated by some imagined affront, or by an accidental one perceived to be intentional, and the counteraffront would be commensurate but real and purposeful, as would be the next and the next and so on. But Harpo is an imp of the perverse, who does everything he wants to, for no other reason than that he is looking for trouble. He gives Chico a loony, almost *conspiratorial* smile, as if he has performed for Chico a necessary or at least a delightful service.

Chico is not delighted.

If this were classic tit-for-tat, he would cut something Harpo values in two. Instead, he pushes Harpo away while saying, "Hey, com'ere." And says to Harpo, against all reason, "Just the guy I wanna see." Bit of a double or triple bind there, but Harpo is unbound. For the sake of connecting this scene, however tangentially, to the movie as a whole, Chico begins grilling Harpo as to whether he has been spying on Firefly.

Harpo's response is to give Chico his leg. This is a thing Harpo started doing in vaudeville and continued to do throughout his life, in any situation. (At a reception in London, however, the Duke of Windsor gave Harpo *his* leg.)

Chico flings Harpo's leg away. Harpo sticks one of the in-the-shell peanuts he stole from Chico into Chico's mouth. Chico spits the peanut out and demands to know why Harpo won't talk. (He hasn't noticed until now that his partner is mute?) Harpo offers Chico a handful of his peanuts. Chico slaps them away. Harpo looks pouty.

"Hey, why you make-a the face?" says Chico, and he pushes Harpo in the face. This provokes Harpo into balling up his fists in a childlike way and taking an aggressive stance. Chico is willing to fight. Harpo fakes with the fists and kicks Chico in the leg.

In what sounds like it might be vintage street-fighting punctilio, Chico says, "Hey, no downstairs. *Up*stairs this time."

By this time we have begun to see Kennedy at his neighboring lemonade stand, but he's busy selling lemonade and has no part in the action so far.

Then Chico pushes Harpo back into a lemonade customer, and the next thing you know, the lemonade dipper is clattering and lemonade is sloshing and the customer is struggling to extricate Harpo's hand from his, the customer's, pants pocket. When he does get Harpo's hand out, Harpo proudly shows him that a piece of paper, maybe money, has come with it. And meanwhile, Harpo is getting his other hand into Kennedy's pants pocket. When Kennedy turns to direct his exasperation toward Chico, he feels a tug and realizes that Harpo has his hand in his, Kennedy's, pocket. Kennedy jerks and slaps and manages to get Harpo's hand out of his pocket, but in the process Harpo pulls the pocket inside out, and he is eyeing it the way he eyed Chico's wiener.

"Hey," blusters Kennedy, "what's the idea?" Indeed. What kind of insane person goes around jamming his hands into other men's pockets? But Kennedy takes offense not at the business with the pockets but at "fighting outside my place and driving my customers away!" While Chico is explaining that *he* wasn't fighting, and giving Kennedy a few kicks to show how Harpo was fighting with *him*, Harpo has his scissors back out and is cutting the pocket out of Kennedy's pants, turning it into a nice little cloth bag, into which he puts some peanuts from his pocket. Perhaps because there is something both symbolic and actual about all this that would seem, to your basic large Irishman, not a good thing to acknowledge, Kennedy does not notice that someone is using his pocket for a nut bag. Kennedy is responding to Chico's explanatory kicks by saying, "Hey, what's the idea?" again.

But he can't stand listening to Chico's explanations, so he addresses some questions to Harpo: "Say, listen, what're you doing around here?"

What he is doing is demonstrating his disregard for Kennedy's personal space. Leaning into Kennedy's paunch, thereby causing the horns he carries in the front of his pants to honk.

"Who are ya?"

Might not these have been questions the boy Harpo had to field when caught on an Irish block?

Again honk.

Chico butts into Kennedy's berating of Harpo by explaining that he and Harpo are spies and casting himself as victim: how is he going to get any spying done if his fellow spy won't talk? Harpo stands by, looking innocent.

"Will you quit annoying me?" Kennedy demands.

All right, says Chico, as long as Kennedy will make Harpo stop kicking Chico in the way that Chico demonstrates by kicking Kennedy. And Harpo gives Kennedy his leg.

That really sets Kennedy off. For *that*, he is going to tear Harpo limb from limb.

Harpo responds by engaging Kennedy in a handshake and knocking both his own hat and Kennedy's to the ground. Kennedy picks up Harpo's hat, Harpo Kennedy's. Chico points out to Kennedy what has happened, and now Kennedy is showing us a great slow burner's slow burn. If this were a Laurel and Hardy movie, both parties to the dispute would be slow burning, but it's a Marx-McCarey movie, so Harpo and Chico aren't slow burning, they're just stoking Kennedy's burn. He's a full head (magnificent big bald head) taller than they are. They're baiting him the way two small dogs might badger an ox.

Harpo seems to offer Kennedy's hat back to him, but instead he takes his own hat back and drops Kennedy's to the ground.

Kennedy, his lips pooched out, bends over to pick up his hat, straightens to put it on, turns to Chico, who is persisting in explaining what his idea is, and Harpo reaches way up (Kennedy being a full head taller than either Marx) and gets his hat in under Kennedy's so that Kennedy winds up wearing Harpo's again and vice versa. For good measure, Harpo gives Kennedy his leg again.

Kennedy sees what Harpo is wearing, realizes what he himself is wearing, utters a gutteral exclamation, and slams Harpo's hat to the ground. Harpo drops Kennedy's hat to the ground. And deftly kicks it away as Kennedy reaches for it.

Then Chico kicks Kennedy's hat back to Harpo, who picks it up and brushes it off, makes to hand it back to him, but then dangles it from an elastic band that happens to be hanging from it, so that when Kennedy stoops to grab it, it bonks him in the face, and when Kennedy does grab it, Harpo gives his foot, in effect, to Kennedy's hat—he's got his foot in Kennedy's hat the way he had his hand in Kennedy's pocket earlier.

A beat. Fume. And Kennedy jerks his hat away from Harpo's foot. Harpo slaps it out of Kennedy's hand back onto the ground.

Now Chico gets more involved. He picks up Kennedy's hat and

puts it on over his own inveterate soft-pointy hat, which looks, does it not, like an inverted lily blossom.

Kennedy looks for his hat on the ground. It's not there. Harpo meanwhile has picked up his own hat and put it on.

Kennedy locates his hat on Chico's head. Takes a beat to wipe sweat from his brow with his sleeve. Removes his and Chico's hats, together, from Chico's head and puts them on his head, not realizing he has put on two hats. Jams 'em on good and firm. Harpo confuses matters by handing Chico his hat.

Kennedy eyes this transaction closely. Can't see anything wrong with it, because he assumes he has his own hat on, which of course he does, but he also has Chico's hat on under it, so when Harpo now removes Kennedy's hat while Kennedy is watching Chico put on Harpo's hat, Kennedy is left with just Chico's hat on. And now Harpo is wearing Kennedy's hat. We have something like a shell game working now, only it's not about Kennedy guessing what shell the pea is under, it's about him trying to figure out where his hat is and which hat he is wearing. It almost amounts to not knowing where his head is.

Looking at Chico, Kennedy senses something is not right. He turns his head, slowly, pensively, toward Harpo.

Sees his hat on Harpo, but can't quite take on board how that can be. Turns back toward Chico. Then begins to turn back toward Harpo (who now has taken Kennedy's hat off and is holding it at chest level), but does a double take toward Chico. Then back toward Harpo, who's in the process of putting Kennedy's hat back on his own head.

Then Harpo brings out the artillery: he throws Kennedy a Gookie.

The Gookie, like so many aspects of the Marx Brothers' performance, went back to their childhood. A man named Gehrke, called Gookie, was a cigar roller in the window of a Lexington Avenue cigar store. He would get so absorbed in his work that his cheeks ballooned and his lips pooched out and his eyes bulged and crossed. Harpo couldn't mimic people's voices like Chico, but he was good at facial expressions. (In this scene, he has already gone through a gamut of them.) He could work on his Gookie imitation by simultaneously staring at Gookie and at his own reflection in the window. When he had Gookie down, he called Gookie's attention to it. Gookie chased him down the street. But Harpo kept coming back. People in the neighborhood started noticing how well Harpo did Gookie. "For the first time, at the age of twelve, I had a reputation. Even Chico began to respect me." Chico would introduce Harpo to people:

> "Shake hands with my brother here. He's the smartest kid in the neighborhood." When the guy put out his hand I'd throw him a Gookie. It always broke up the poolroom.

Confronted with a Gookie, Kennedy lurches away, toward the camera, with his own cheeks puffed out and lips jammed together—not in imitation but out of frustration—and then on back toward Chico, who is doing a low-grade Gookie of his own. (I never noticed this until just now, going through frame by frame.) Kennedy lurches back the other way, but then double takes back toward Chico, covers his face with his hands, turns back toward Harpo, who is holding his Gookie (Chico's Gookie has faded); then (notice that that was the first semicolon I have resorted to in regard to this scene) Kennedy does a quick little stutter take; and Chico's hand is going back up to Harpo's hat on his head, and I'm thinking the intricate gag breaks down at this point in the take, because the next frame is shot from farther back.

Chico still has Harpo's hat on, and Kennedy is fuming at Chico—who, I see now, is semi-Gookie-ing again—and Harpo is snatching Chico's hat off Kennedy's head and putting it on his own head and passing Kennedy's hat to Chico, who puts it on his own head and hands Harpo's hat to Kennedy, and while Kennedy is holding Harpo's hat and staring at Chico donning his, Kennedy's, hat, Harpo takes his own hat from Kennedy and puts Chico's hat on Kennedy's head.

Only no—Chico's hat never quite gets fully onto Kennedy's head this time, because while Kennedy is fumbling with it, trying to keep it off his head, Chico grabs it and replaces it with Kennedy's hat.

Now everybody's got the right hat on. But Kennedy is still trying to collect his wits. When Harpo reaches out toward Kennedy's leg, Kennedy unaccountably gives it to him. When Kennedy realizes what he has done, he is further horrified, takes his leg back, and reaches back to throw a punch at Harpo, but Chico takes that opportunity to give Kennedy his, Chico's, leg. Kennedy rejects Chico's leg, lunges at Chico, and chases him out of the frame. Harpo takes this moment to fill up one of his rubber-bulb horns with lemonade from Kennedy's stand and to put the horn through his belt in such a way that when Kennedy—bursting back into the frame with no Chico and much vexation—collides with Harpo, lemonade squirts up into his face.

"Why you!" Not much of a rejoinder on Kennedy's part, but let us not, unless we have ever found ourselves in such a set of circumstances, be quick to judge.

And again, another belly bump squirts Kennedy in the face.

Kennedy covers his face with his hands as Harpo beams. If Chico's grin is engaging, how would you describe Harpo's beams? Demented, yes. Morally indifferent, maybe. But not really in a *bad* way.

And then, slowly, wetly, Kennedy begins to laugh, a slow deep *heh-heh* and then *HAH-HAH* Victor McLaglen kind of laugh, and Harpo silently shares it with him, even slaps Kennedy on the shoulder, both of them having a hearty guffaw—and finally Kennedy scores a point: he grabs the lemonade-filled horn from Harpo's belt, and as Harpo is deep into an eyes-shut, mouth-wide-open silent belly laugh, Kennedy turns the horn around and squirts it down inside the front of Harpo's pants.

Several times. And Harpo's expression changes. He gets a horrified, lemonade-down-the-pants look. Kennedy throws him a double take and then heads off toward Chico again. Harpo, standing in a big puddle, screws up his face in a sort of defensive semi-Gookie and minces off camera, whistling and shaking each leg in turn, moist by his own petard.

I say, moist by his own . . .

GROUCHO AND CHICO: Go right ahead. Don't mind us.

We may be reminded that Harpo was so nervous the first time he went onstage in the family vaudeville act that he wet his pants. We may also think of the lovely woman in a nice black silky dress who happens to be walking down the street in the vicinity of the all-time-great pie-throwing orgy in *Battle of the Century,* the Laurel and Hardy silent that McCarey supervised. She steps in a splattered pie, slips, sits down on the pie, registers an obscure befoulment, rises, and walks off in a gingerly, *ick*-expressive, picking-at-her-backside, shake-a-leg way.

And now Kennedy is accosting Chico, by the peanut stand: "I'll teach you to kick me."

"You don't have to teach me, I already know how" (so much for progressive education), says Chico as he kicks Kennedy in such a way that Kennedy's hat flies off and Harpo, entering, catches it and puts it on the peanut-stand burner and taps Kennedy on the back and whistles and points at the hat so Kennedy can watch it burn up. As Kennedy himself slow burns.

And Chico says what I couldn't get him or Groucho to say about "moist by his own petard."

"Ah," says Chico. " 'At's-a good, eh?"

All that in four minutes and thirteen seconds.

Does any of this advance the plot? No. But none of it seems dragged in either. McCarey's theory of construction, he told Bog-danovich, was "the ineluctability of incidents. The idea is that if something happens, some other thing inevitably flows from it—like night follows day . . . I always develop my stories that way, in a series of incidents that succeed and provoke each other. I never really have intrigues."*

Exactly what this movie doesn't have: intrigue, which is to say,

---

* "The lack of reason," writes David Thomson, "is suited to the arbitrariness of the screen and its ability to unfold events which one can do nothing to stop or control. Anything can be put on the screen from one frame to the next and its appearance will do away with the need for explanation. The Marx Brothers' films rely more than most on this autonomy, and Harpo more than any of his brothers."

plotting, which is to say, plodding. Trentino and Miss Vera Marcal try to scheme, but the Marxes are a series of chain reactions, too fast to be strategized against; they expose machinations as mechanical. Much of *Duck Soup*'s volatility derives from the Marxes themselves, but none of their other movies flows like this one, like shining from shook foil that keeps on shaking. We may recall Vera's warning to Trentino early on, "It may not be so ee-see." Not for him, it won't, but for the Marxes: duck soup.

But the consistency of this movie is not only propulsive, it is also thematic. This is a family drama, a true bromance: brothers constantly rubbing each other the wrong way and giving each other a hard time but then rallying together when faced with a much larger opponent: Mrs. Teasdale, Trentino, Kennedy, Sylvania. And let us not forget that Groucho always called *Duck Soup* "the war movie." (In 2007 *Military History* magazine picked *Duck Soup* as the twenty-seventh greatest war movie of all time, ahead of *The Deer Hunter, Schindler's List, Pork Chop Hill, The Story of G.I. Joe, Battleship Potemkin, From Here to Eternity,* and *A Bridge Too Far.*) What is war but tit-for-tat?

Back to the story line. In the script, Trentino exits and Firefly shouts down to Chico. They bandy lines back and forth about Chico's dog. Of these jokes, the only one that survives in the movie is the pun on *license* and *lice*. (The others are pretty bad—Chico says that when he calls the dog he whistles "Yankee Poodle.") Groucho invites Chico to continue the conversation inside.

The telephone-grabbing stuff (Identity Issue alert) is in Kalmar-Ruby. The Chico-Groucho riddling back and forth (a swirl of Identity Issues) is better in the film than in the script. In the script, Groucho's ulterior motive—specifically, selling ammunition—is a prominent factor. Chico, who becomes Secretary of War in the script more or less as haphazardly as in the film (but it's snappier in the film), says in the script that he doesn't want any ammunition because there is no war, so Groucho says they'll start one, and he asks Chico's advice. Got to insult somebody, Chico says. So Groucho insults Chico. No, no, got to insult somebody from another country. How about Trentino.

All so sane and venal, in the script. In the movie, Groucho is not trying to sell anything or to save the country. Aside from figuring out that the answer to the riddle Chico poses him is, insultingly, himself,* Groucho's is a higher purpose: to hold on to a position in which he can keep on making irresponsible wisecracks. If he loses that position, all the brothers are out of their jobs and the movie will have to start making sense in terms other than its own. And Trentino, because he is wooing Mrs. Teasdale with an eye to taking over the country (who cares about the country, but we need that straight lady), is a threat. Zeppo, who is far more outspoken than in previous movies, tells Groucho, "The man is trying to undermine you. Now what are you going to do about it?"

The idea, let us bear in mind, is to provoke Trentino into leaving the country. Nothing more. So far.

But first, a word about Harpo's flashing of tattoos. In the script, it begins when Harpo is still passing himself off as a prospective female spy and continues after his girl parts deflate. And the last tattoo is not of a doghouse with a real dog emerging to bark, as we see in the film, but of an outhouse with "the head of a real man" appearing in the opening, "terribly angry at being interrupted."

---

* In case you're interested, the French subtitle translates "a big pain in the neck" into *vraiment casse-pieds,* which I believe is literally "truly a feet-breaker."

In 1933 there was no Production Code to command that revision. Just, I suppose, someone's taste. Whose? McCarey's? Mankiewicz's? Whoever's idea the revision was, it is not surprising, I think. I have wracked my memory of pre-Code movies, and surprising as it may seem today, I am forced to conclude that sophistication then did not extend to potty jokes. Not waggishness but just practicality—he practiced once a day—caused Harpo to keep his harp next to the toilet at home.

Let's have a hand for the gag with Harpo and his scissors going out and Zeppo coming in wearing half a hat. Did I mention that this is Zeppo's last movie? He looks good in half a hat. Funny stuff happening offscreen is another McCarey trademark. In *The Awful Truth*, for instance, a long and loud fistfight between Cary Grant and a man he thinks has been fooling around with his estranged wife goes on out of sight.

McCarey was also known for his hat gags. I'm not saying that the Marx Brothers and their various writers couldn't come up with hat business, but McCarey's movies are full of them. See Cary Grant studying himself in the mirror in *The Awful Truth*. His derby doesn't quite fit. How can that be. New hat. It fit when he wore it into this very same room. Sloowwlly it dawns on him. It's not his hat. It's the hat of the man he suspects of dallying with his estranged wife, Irene Dunne. The aforementioned fistfight ensues.

It was McCarey who put scissors in Harpo's hands for this movie. We might see a reckless pair of scissors as an homage to the brothers' dad, Frenchie, the improvisational tailor, who never measured before he cut.

But enough of this trivia! We have an incident to provoke. Firefly arrives at Mrs. T's garden party, carrying, note, a single glove.

(In the script, there are two of them, and they're called gauntlets. Too obvious.)

You're wondering what the French is for "a Rufus over your head," aren't you? Since I have watched this movie with the French subtitle option provided by the DVD, I can tell you. In French, Groucho's name isn't Rufus T. Firefly. It is Antoine Luciole. *Luciole* is French for firefly, but why *Antoine*? *Solely for the sake of this pun.* When Mrs. T says, "Oh, Rufus!" and he says, "All I can offer you is a roofus over your head," the French subtitles are, "Oh, Antoine," and *"Je peux vous juste offrir un An-toit-ne sur votre tête."*

Groucho's character's name has been changed solely to put a *toit* in it. I can't say for sure, but I don't think it's as funny in French.

The roofus joke is in the Kalmar-Ruby script. But in the script Groucho doesn't get around to calling Trentino a baboon. His interruption of Trentino's wooing of Mrs. T, and his suggestion that when Trentino gets finished with being at her feet he perform some chiropody on Groucho's,* is enough to make Trentino call him, as in the film, a swine. (*Saligaud.*) A worm. (*Larve.*) And then, finally, an upstart! (*Arriviste.*) *Swine* and *worm* are like water off a duck's back, but for Firefly *upstart* tears it, inasmuch as, he maintains, Fireflies came over on the *Mayflower* (with horseflies on them).

These days, when *start-up* has a positive entrepreneurial ring, *upstart* may seem too obviously ludicrous, but in the thirties there was still enough old-line stuffiness around to lend the term some sting. To insult a Marx brother by calling him an upstart, however, would be like calling Mother Teresa a bleeding heart or

---

* In the script there's a line about not having seen his chiropodist in years. Don't forget that Groucho had once aspired to a career in chiropody.

Andy Warhol an arty type and expecting them to take offense. Upstarts the Marxes were proud to be. And very American it was of them too.

Both of the brothers' parents, Minnie and Frenchie, were born in Germany, and they arrived in America with no money or social position. The brothers presumed their way up from there to wealth and fame, mocking the pretensions of the well-born all along the way. In *Monkey Business* (as in *Night at the Opera*) they are shipboard stowaways. At one point Chico confuses *mutinies* and *matinees,* and Groucho, who has slipped into the captain's quarters and donned the captain's coat and hat, exclaims, "There's my argument. Restrict immigration." But that was Groucho onscreen, forever trying to dissociate himself from that rabble, his brothers. In life he was ambivalent about himself and pretty much everything else and was famous for remarks such as, when told he couldn't swim in the pool of a restricted country club,* "My daughter is only half

* Groucho made his famous joke that he wouldn't belong to any club that would have him in a letter to the Friars Club announcing his resignation because he was seldom in New York anymore and didn't use the membership. In Hollywood he was a regular at the Hillcrest Country Club, which was restricted to Jews until Harpo, by his account, led a campaign to de-restrict it. McCarey belonged to the Lakeside Country Club, which was restricted to non-Jews. In her review of *Hannah and Her Sisters,* in which *Duck Soup* inspires the Woody Allen character not to off himself, Pauline Kael complained that Allen had in fact gotten away from his early, heavily Marx-influenced strengths to fall back on conventional Upper West Side of Manhattan cultural values: "He has found a club that will have him." Pauline duly appreciated *Duck Soup* and the Marxes (when asked what movies she'd like to see again, she would cite *Duck Soup* and *Million-Dollar Legs,* a W. C. Fields vehicle produced by Mankiewicz), but she had a soft spot for the Ritz Brothers, whom most critics hold up as vastly inferior. (The Ritzes are in fact terrific in *On the Avenue.*) I have a photo of Pauline at lunch with, and making a face comparable to a Gookie with, Harry Ritz. She told me she had lunch with Groucho, in his old age, and prevailed upon him to go say hello to Dean Martin, who was at another table with a blonde or two. Dino cut Groucho dead.

Jewish—can she go in up to her waist?" But he flaunted his humble background, knowing it to be comedy gold.

In an article, "Smile Stranger," in *Literature/Film Quarterly*, Mark Winokur writes that the Marxes act out "the tension about placement between two cultures" and that they "honor their parents by dishonoring the culture they've been thrust into." This is not just recalcitrant but heroic, a refusal to give in to what Winokur calls "the shame that the second-generation child feels for his parents . . . superseded periodically by the shame he feels for rejecting them." The Marxes "evade assimilation into or segregation from the dominant culture by creating official roles for themselves which they then allow their immigrant sub-personae to subvert." So *haute* America looks at us through its lorgnette—

> **GROUCHO:** Are you lorgnette?
>
> **CHICO:** Nah. Sometimes I'm-a lone, but I ain't lorn yet.
>
> **GROUCHO:** And no hoity-toity ambassador is going to lorn us a thing or two neither.

—and finds us strange? We'll dress up in top hats and swallowtails too, ratty ones, and we'll show you *strange*.

Winokur compares Groucho's wisecracking to the rat-a-tat snarls and tommy-gun fire of ethnic gangster types in movies of the period. But the gangsters, in their gaudy and violent ways, are desperately trying to get a piece of the American pie. The Marxes, he points out, are not "trying to gain entry to the mainstream."

They have stronger juice than the mainstream, and they're squirting it in all directions. *Arriviste* indeed! They have arrived.*

But affecting to be deeply affronted gets Groucho's juices flowing, and here we go tit-for-tat. The stated purpose of insulting Trentino, you may recall, was only to get him to leave Freedonia, not to bring Freedonia and Sylvania to the brink of war. But Firefly has his face-slapping glove with him, and one thing has a way of leading to another.

In the script, Miss Marcal tries to intervene between Firefly and Trentino. "You can't do this!" she says.

Trentino rebuffs her: "War is not a woman's problem."

"It is every woman's problem," she responds angrily. "Who supplies the sons?—the brothers?—the husbands?"

Uh-oh. Are the writers getting *serious* here? Miss M's scripted speech may have been inspired by an Irving Berlin song that Groucho liked to sing in performance, no doubt in part because Berlin himself hated it so much that, he told Groucho, "if you ever have an urge to sing that song again, if you'll get in touch with me, I'll give you a hundred dollars not to sing it." Berlin was moved to write that song by the First World War. The Devil is telling his son about people on earth: "They're breaking the hearts of mothers, / They're making butchers out of brothers." That sentiment, Groucho opined during the Vietnam War, when *Duck Soup* was enjoying a revival

---

* I don't know what generation Irish-American McCarey was, but his immigrant juices were less fresh than the Marxes'. His father, who had been a big-time boxing promoter in Los Angeles, made enough money to send his son, against his will, to law school. McCarey did not last long as a lawyer. When he turned against his own client, on ample grounds of taste, the client chased him out of the courthouse and down the street. McCarey fled past an acquaintance, who said, "What are you doing?" "Practicing law," said McCarey.

among antiwar youth, "applies today just as much as it did forty years ago."

In the script, Firefly is all about business, not peace. He interrupts Miss Marcal: "You keep that up and you'll crab the whole war." And to Trentino, "How're ya fixed for ammunition?"

Back to war writ small. That's a nice-looking dog Chico has, isn't it? *Pastrami*'s a nice name for him.* What could be nicer than a nice fella with a nice dog and a nice small trade in peanuts? And a fella has to take a break every now and then, but it would have been wiser to leave Pastrami in charge of the stand instead of Harpo. Because Edgar Kennedy shows up. Wearing a nice new hat. Straw, this time. Immediately we know what must happen to that hat. The escalation that leads to what must happen to that hat, happens: peanuts, mustard, sash, scissors, more peanuts, and now that nice new hat is burning (as we knew it would be, and if we feel bad for the hat, and for its owner, as perhaps in

---

* Personally I am glad that the following dialogue in the script did not make it to the screen. After Chico avoids saying what his dog's name is, Groucho persists: "How do you call your dog when you want him?" "I *don't* want him," says Chico. The script is often harsh to animals. At one point Harpo, at the sight of a mouse, is called upon to produce a mousetrap, get down on the floor and whistle, and draw the mouse into the trap, which snaps on him. We don't want to see Harpo picking on little mice. Edgar Kennedy is a much more suitable outlet for aggression. Harpo and animals worked well together—the most nuanced performance I have ever seen a seal give in a motion picture is in *At the Circus*. Harpo is playing checkers. The seal is kibitzing, giving Harpo pointed nudges. Thanks to the seal, Harpo's opponent jumps all of his checkers in one fell swoop. Harpo gives the seal a reproachful look. A beat. The seal shrugs, Harpo gives the seal a big forgiving smile and nuzzle. Kalmar-Ruby's antagonism toward animals wouldn't have suited even Groucho. In an early draft of a script they wrote for *The Big Store*, Groucho interrupts a man who is beating a dog—"Don't hit her, she's man's best friend." The dog bites Groucho in the rear. "Go ahead," he says, "beat the hell out of her." Kalmar and Ruby gave us lovely love songs, and they were better writers of primo Marxian comedy than their literary superior, S. J. Perelman. But they had a coarse streak.

fact we do, then we are too soft for this game), and the peanut stand is overturned.

Downer. So it's up to Harpo. Harpo with his pants rolled up, like Groucho's at the gala. "Of course," David Thomson writes about *The Man with a Movie Camera,* "the film is full of tricks and editing but they are all as candid and innocent as someone warning you that he's going to cheat you." Every move of lovable Harpo is a warning. *Upstart* isn't the half of it: the man will stop at nothing. To slosh bare-legged in a lemonade vendor's lemonade is to impose even more egregiously than when you handed him your thigh or entangled your hand in his pocket or wiped mustard on his sash or leaned against him, belly to belly, to honk your horn. Harpo is not standoffish. As Raymond Durgnat puts it, "He steals things like a baby grasps an adult's nose to play with. Like a baby, he tries to eat inedibles, especially telephones,* and being a magic baby, invariably succeeds." To a baby, one may suppose, lemonade is a treat to get your legs into. Harpo told the *Saturday Evening Post* that he never liked lemonade until he discovered in *Duck Soup* that it was "wonderful when properly used."

Can big war be averted? "Not if His Excellency will listen to reason." Another of my favorite lines. There need be no war, says Trentino, if Firefly will only behave like other deranged dictators and be rational.

To that end, Mrs. T calls Firefly over to her place, and he arrives (with a glove in his breast pocket for some reason), and the two of them put their heads together, literally. When they're temple to temple, looking forward to utterly notional married days, it

---

* That happens in *The Cocoanuts.* He also eats a bellboy's buttons and drinks ink.

is actually kind of sweet, isn't it? War, schmar, Mrs. T is in love. Unlike many straitlaced characters, she is by no means an awkward figure. She is much more comfortable in her skin, or at any rate her clothes, than Groucho is. And yet, she is touched by his attentions. If she were not bottomlessly, rechargeably gullible, the way he behaves toward her might well fail to amuse. Don't we *like* to see her big happy smile? (The extent to which she is a Minnie Marx figure that the boys can push around, as opposed to one who pushed the boys around, awaits consideration.) I don't know about you, but I'm freeze framing that smile for a while. We are fully aware that Groucho is going to pull the rug from under that smile, but she, Ms. Dumont, is not. Bless her. Maybe I should want her to shake Groucho by the scruff of the neck and say, "Listen here, Your Excellency, stop being crazy. You're about to drive us to war."

But I don't want her to. I trust her to enable, in the face of all reason, this comedy.

Is she in on the joke? The real question is whether she's in on the seriousness. How can she keep translating the insults against her into harmless kidding? Such a good smile, and Groucho keeps dispelling it, and it bounces back when he asks for a lock of her hair, and she says, "A lock of my heh-ah?" (or however you would spell the way she pronounces *hair*), and then he says, "I'm letting you off easy. I was going to ask for the whole wig."

Oof. Is *Duck Soup* misogynist? The Marx Brothers (except for Chico at the piano) do tend to appeal less to women than to men. Speaking demographically, I will venture to say that many, many women these days would push aside *Duck Soup* in favor of *Mamma Mia*, which I once watched, horror-stricken, in a hotel room. I cite *Mamma Mia* because it has several parallels to *Duck Soup*. Frankly,

I forget the details. If you insist, I will go back and watch *Mamma Mia* again—but basically, it moves as constantly as *Duck Soup,* its protagonists are three or four sibling-esh women . . .

Why did I even bring this up? Instead, we could be focusing on a joke that comes in here somewhere and holds up well today: Firefly can't call off the war, he says, because it's too late, he has already paid a month's rent on the battlefield. The military-industrial complex writ small, you might say—but remember, this is not so much an antiwar movie as a dance to the music of belligerence.

Belligerence and prejudice. Here comes the one blatantly politically incorrect one-liner of *Duck Soup,* the one moment when the laughing New York City children and young parents with whom I watched the movie at the Thalia fell silent.

"Isn't there something I can do?" asks Miss Vera Marcal, and okay, Groucho does give her a flicker of sidelong lust, but we know he won't follow it up. (Zeppo would, but he is probably off somewhere weaving the halves of his straw hat back together.)

"Maybe I am a little headstrong," says Firefly, "but I come by it honestly. My father was a little headstrong. My mother was a little Armstrong. The Headstrongs married the Armstrongs, and that's why darkies were born."

(*"Un Tetu a epousé une Costaud et c'est de la que viennent les negros."*)

Okay. Two years before *Duck Soup* appeared, a fat, hearty white person named Kate Smith, in her day the biggest lady of radio-floated popular song, got high up onto the charts with a song called "That's Why Darkies Were Born." I have not been able to find any recording of that performance online. In the same year, Paul Robeson, an eminently serious African American, recorded the same song, and that version is listenable online. Its drift, which is congruent with "Old Man River," which Robeson sang in the first movie version of *Showboat,* is that somebody had to pick the cotton and "laugh at trouble," given that white people (presumably) weren't up to it. No doubt about it, the sentiment is terrible: that black people's existence is justified by what white people couldn't do, or didn't want to do.

And I am not aware of anything that either McCarey or any Marx brother did specifically for racial equality, though Groucho and Harpo were liberal Democrats. (Chico or Zeppo, who knows?) According to Stefan Kanfer's biography of Groucho, all four of them had "rued the days of segregated vaudeville" and were "appalled when the Daughters of American Revolution denied the black singer Marian Anderson the use of its auditorium."

But I can't think of any black people in Marx Brothers movies except for the bearers who have carried Captain Spaulding all the way from Africa in *Animal Crackers;* a glimpse of Willie Best, bug-eyed, as a porter in *At the Circus;* and singers and dancers in *A Day at the Races* and *At the Circus.* Simon Louvish decries the "mawkish and bizarre" scene of Harpo in *A Day at the Races* (no pun intended) tootling a flute and playing " 'Gabriel' to a strange community of shack-dwelling blacks which seems to have sprung up," a scene that "labors the point of Harpo as an elf for all races, a soul mate for the dispossessed." There is that aspect, and there are unpleasant close-ups of wide-eyed African Americans asking, "Who dat man?"

But most of that number consists of rousing African-American singing and swing dancing, including the only movie appearance of the elegantly twinkle-eyed Ivie Anderson laying down "All God's

Chillun Got Rhythm."* As it happens, that number was the only part of any Marx Brothers movie to be nominated for an Oscar (for dance direction). When the Marxes see the sheriff coming for them, they black up their faces (Harpo, only the left side of his) with axle grease and mingle with the dancing. They hold their own well enough for middle-aged white boys.

Also problematic is the "Swingali" number in *At the Circus*, in which Harpo is again a kind of spell-casting juju-man. Stefan Kanfer complains, not without reason, that "the chorus in Harpo's number is composed almost entirely of . . . the kind of wide-eyed, grinning exaggerations who disfigured . . . *A Day at the Races*." But among the musicians are serious-looking little kids, with whom Harpo interacts eye to eye. It's all very broad, God knows—but if there ever was a wide-eyed grinning exaggeration, or an innocent-babe blank-looking exaggeration, or a squinch-eyed scowling exaggeration, or a slack-jawed befuddled exaggeration, it's Harpo exaggerating himself. If Harpo is burning in hell for racial insensitivity, then the afterlife isn't fair.

At any rate, nobody holds anything against Harpo. Leo McCarey's politics is another matter. In the fifties,[†] he was anti-Communist to the point that he testified as a friendly—but evidently not name-naming—

---

* Dorothy Dandridge, fourteen years old, is said to be among the dancers, but I don't know that anyone has identified which one she is. My bet is that she is one of the two fleetingly seen girls in white blouses and gray jumpers. (Might the other one be her sister, Vivian? The two of them and Etta James were a trio calling themselves the Dandridge Sisters at the time.) Members of Duke Ellington's band, way uncredited, are said to be among the musicians.

† One reason probably for his critical neglect. But his last two movies, *Rally 'Round the Flag, Boys!* and *Satan Never Sleeps*, were awful by any standard, and so on the whole was *Once Upon a Honeymoon* (1942), and *Good Sam* (1948) wasn't much better. His best comedies, however, are finer than Capra's.

witness before the witch-hunting House Un-American Activities Committee. His movies didn't make money in the Soviet Union, he told the committee. "I think I have a character in there that they do not like."

"Bing Crosby?"

"No, God."

In 1951 McCarey made a documentary, *You Can Change the World,* in which tribute is paid to anti-Red Americanism by an actual Catholic priest and Bing Crosby, Jack Benny, William Holden, Bob Hope, and just about the only black man who might, with a stretch, have been called a movie star at the time, Eddie "Rochester" Anderson. In 1952 McCarey directed a joltingly anti-liberal feature film, *My Son John.** It was Mae West, not McCarey, though he was duly appreciative, who insisted on involving Duke Ellington and his orchestra in *Belle of the Nineties.*

If you want to wince at something racist in a fun 1933 movie, try *Footlight Parade,* which features some of Busby Berkeley's most kaleidoscopic numbers. As the musical director trying to come up with a concept for one of those numbers, Jimmy Cagney sees black kids playing in an open fire hydrant and has an epiphany: "I've got it! A crystal-pure waterfall playing over beautiful white bodies."

Online you can join in discussions of just how disappointed we should feel, or how much we should forgive ourselves for not feeling, about *Duck Soup* because of its *d*-word joke. That joke is a dead spot today, and Groucho would doubtless have thrown it out by now—in Groucho's aesthetic, if they don't laugh, it's no

---

* Robert Warshow called it "an attack on Communism and an affirmation of American-ism that might legitimately alarm any thoughtful American whether liberal or conser-vative."

good. But you *could* say he was making edgy fun of a dumb song, couldn't you?

Mince! (Which I gather from a *Duck Soup* subtitle is French for *Gosh!*) Yes, you could.

Firefly says "Gosh" because he can't even remember which of Trentino's insults so outraged him. All four parties chuckle together as Trentino helpfully runs through the list. Worm? Swine? *Anh-anh,* says Groucho. "No, it was a seven-letter word."

Let us pause, if we may, to acknowledge the genius of Groucho's perversity here. Not only is he encouraging the now-jovial Trentino to recollect the casus belli, he is archly giving him hints. All this is in the script, but look how Groucho sells it.

And Trentino comes up with *upstart* again, and Groucho slaps him with his trusty glove, presumably brought along for this purpose. Trentino declares Groucho to be "impossible," and war inevitable, and Groucho tops that with a snappy towel joke.

UOH! cries Mrs. T.

Madness! How can a run-of-the-mill snake like Trentino intrigue against slipperiness so unabashed? He can't. He would have to be Harpo and Chico. But Trentino persists—he's got Miss Marcal at Mrs. T's house looking for Freedonia's war plans, which "I happen to know" are in Mrs. T's possession.

In the script he happens to know because Miss Marcal (oh, let's start calling her Vera) has overheard Firefly stashing the plans with her. Next, in the script, Trentino bumps into Harpo at the opera (!) and tells him that Mrs. T has the plans. Chico appears to know this already, because he is sitting next to Mrs. T and getting too familiar with her for her taste and mine, because she is sitting on her purse, which has the plans in it. Meanwhile, Harpo produces a bow and arrow and shoots several apples off the head of William Tell's son before Tell himself can do it, and he produces a fishing rod and baits a hook with "a real live worm" and casts into an onstage pool and catches a carp. Then, with a hand from Chico, he catches the purse.

A Night at the Opera is funnier than that. And so is what replaces, in *Duck Soup* as shot, all this scripted snatching and grabbing. Kalmar and Ruby have Groucho and Vera dancing ballet together. Vera has the plans in her bodice, and Groucho tries to dip her deeply enough to dislodge it. (In *At the Circus*, Eve Arden, playing an acrobat, has $10,000 hidden in her bodice, and Groucho talks her into walking on the ceiling with suction-cup shoes so it will drop out.) Chico and Harpo join in, and "a four-cornered adagio" ensues.

Let us return to the movie as made. We are just over halfway through it now, most of the best stuff is coming up, and almost none of it is in the script. What's coming was partly worked out at McCarey's beach house and partly improvised on the set. The proportions, we don't know. But we do know this:

People think of Marx Brothers movies as impromptu, but most of them, before and after *Duck Soup*, were hammered out onstage, on the road, before being shot. Tight as it is, *Duck Soup*—directed by a master of improv inducement who was also a walking repository of silent-movie gags—is their freshest confection.

Harpo and Chico are still Sylvanian agents, even though the latter is Freedonia's Secretary of War. So they have to steal the war plans. The two of them and the servant who answers the door at Mrs. Teasdale's mansion go through an old in-and-out routine, virtually silent. According to Wes D. Gehring's critical biography of McCarey, he had supervised less elaborate versions of this business in 1925 (*Fighting Fluid,* with Charlie Chase) and 1928 (*Early to Bed,* with Laurel and Hardy). The boys can't engage in espionage like grown-ups, or even like rational beings. (But then, have you ever read a novel by John le Carré?) Harpo rings the bell and hides from Chico behind the same hedge Chico was just hiding from him behind, which might not seem very clever—but ah, Harpo has his fingers crossed!

Miss Marcal lets them in, and would you get a load of what she is wearing now? A negligee (with furry short sleeves, perhaps Persian cat) that she has to *hold together in front* with one hand at all times. And yes, Harpo does for the moment take almost-sufficient cognizance of her charms: jumps straight up in the air and then in one fluid motion (comprising two shots, one from outside and one from in) runs headlong into her, grabs her in a bear hug, and foxtrots her into the parlor. God knows how she manages to preserve her modesty, not to mention her balance: note that she is holding the long train of her garment up with her *other* hand.

She also retains presence of mind. The boys are here for spying, not amour. "Whatever you do, don't make a sound," she says. "If you're found, you're lost." Of course that's a big fat verbal softball for Chico. But consider the scenes in Mrs. T's house, all the shushing and clangor of them, in the context of movie history. In 1933 the industry was just emerging from the transition portrayed in that other great comedy, *Singin' in the Rain:* sound pictures were still wet behind the ears. As late as mid-1930, Hollywood studios had still been producing their films in silent as well as sound versions. Sound technology was still presenting technical problems that tended to constrain the spontaneity and fluidity of film comedy. In 1934 comedy would begin going screwball: some slapstick, yes, but mostly snappy patter. McCarey had learned his trade in the silent era. Harpo—no wonder McCarey was so fond of him—was the only nontalker left.

"Remember," insists Vera, "whatever you do, *don't make a sound*." Which means they will be making—although almost wordlessly—a great deal of clatter. If the cinema, in 1933, had just come screechingly indeterminate out of a soundless tunnel, in Mrs. T's house that traumatic switch is rethrown over and over. Rather than shut down the clock, Harpo resets it so that it rings out at midnight. He picks up a music box and at first tries to turn it off but then begins to dance to it as he plucks the strings on the handy piano.

This passing lick is so poignantly vestigial that I can't help interrupting the flow of events to point out how poignantly vestigial this passing lick is. In any other Marx Brothers movie, Harpo would himself have interrupted the action at this point, to lose himself in arpeggios. Before and after *Duck Soup,* the Marxes' movies featured not only intermittent cooing and crooning by vapid young couples but also musical solos by Chico, on piano, and Harpo, on harp. There were two Harpos in the movies, Harpo said in his memoir: the crazy one you see mugging and running around, and the one you see at the harp. The Harpo at the harp, said Harpo, was Harpo. As a child, he had fixated on the harp that his grandmother Fanny Schoenberg brought over from the old country. By the time he was a teenager he was performing publicly on his own harp. In retirement he progressed to playing the music of *Arnold* Schoenberg, no relation.

So for his own and also for Chico's sake, he can't pass up the chance to strum the piano. Although he may be shot for it! And now more racket as the piano top whangs down on his hands. As we see here briefly, Harpo's hands themselves are highly expressive dramatic instruments. (Whereas in other movies, Chico's right hand—dancing on a keyboard, twiddling confidently for our attention and shooting the keys—is more than an instrument, it's a character.)

Got to get Groucho involved. Where is he? Mrs. T entreats him by phone to "come over here," which sounds like he's in another house, but no, because here comes Chico sneaking into his bedroom and locking him in the bathroom. "Hey, let me out of here, or throw me a magazine." (Okay, one potty joke.) The important thing is, Groucho is wearing a nightgown. So Chico can disguise himself as Groucho in every particular but the accent, and even for that he has an explanation: he's practicing up maybe he goes to Italy sometime.

Independently Harpo decides to don a Groucho costume too. You might think Mrs. T would pick up on how much more loosely than Groucho Harpo does the Groucho walk. Or that she would at least *suspect* he is not Groucho when she asks, after giving him the combination to the safe that the plans are in, "Is there anything else you want to know?" and instead of snapping at her (in the beat-repetitive-beat structure that his writers felt was unnecessarily redundant but that Groucho knew the laughing audience's level of cognizance required) something like, I don't know, this—

GROUCHO: Do I wanna know anything you might know that I don't know? No.

But no, Harpo silently tilts toward her bosom and honks the horn he has under his nighty. And as far as Mrs. T can tell, Pinky is "Your Excellency." In all due respect, we may say that Margaret Dumont, or at least Mrs. T, is not a highly intuitive person, thank God.

Quick platonic-bedroom-farce shuffle of Chico-as-Groucho, Harpo-as-Groucho, and Groucho-as-Groucho, about which not much needs to be said other than Chico's famous question to Mrs. T, "Who you gonna believe, me or your own eyes?"*

Now that he has the safe's combination, it's back to the parlor for Harpo—sliding on his sock feet in a way that may have inspired Tom Cruise's doorway sock hopping in *Risky Business*. But Harpo's slide evokes youthful abandon better than Cruise's preeny dance.

Again silent Harpo unleashes traumatic sound. What he takes to be the safe becomes a radio that won't stop blaring "Stars and Stripes Forever," although Harpo does to it everything that strikes him as called for—squirts it with seltzer and dashes it to pieces.† Harpo hears Groucho coming. He runs headlong, for some reason

---

* You probably don't remember this, no reason you should, but back there when Harpo was plaguing Edgar Kennedy at the peanut stand, I mentioned that Harpo had cut off Kennedy's pocket and made a little peanut bag from it. In an earlier draft of this commentary, however, I wrote this: "Don't we hope he will work that little bag into the scene? Fill it with peanuts maybe? According to a shooting script published by Simon & Schuster, 'built up from a dialogue continuity provided by Universal City Studios, Inc., amplified with material gained from a shot-to-shot viewing of [the] film,' Harpo 'starts happily filling the amputated pocket with peanuts.' But that's not on the DVD. I want a small bagful of my money back." That's what I wrote. Then it occurred to me to see whether the pocket filling was on the VHS version, so I watched that, and *aha!*, it was, so I thought, there's an interesting discrepancy, and I went back to the DVD, and *uh-oh*, it was there too. Despite my adamantine previous belief that it wasn't. So don't take my word as gospel about anything you see in this movie. I know I don't.

† We might wonder whether Harpo had just been listening to Hitler on the radio.

(you'd think he'd see himself coming), into a big full-length mirror and dashes *it* to pieces.

And here we go. The mirror scene.

Freeze, please, because this scene warrants introduction. From *Snow White* to *Taxi Driver,* and including *Fearless Vampire Killers, Illusion of Life, The Lady from Shanghai, Duplicity, Dark Passage, The Earrings of Madame de . . .* —we all have a list, don't we, of mirror shots in movies.* What does any camera produce but a mirror image, flopped?

But what we are about to watch now is *the* mirror scene. The routine had predecessors, and it has often been copied, but this is the copper-plumbing standard. Three minutes and fifty seconds not only without dialogue but—which is not always evident in a laugh-filled theater—entirely soundless. A hush falls. Two brothers, in nightgowns, dance, as one. It is absurd. It can't be happening. It is a beautiful thing. Let's watch it now, and talk about it after.

Were you with someone? I went downstairs and got my wife and watched it with her. It was her severalth time, my twentieth or thirtieth. It was still good. I am tempted, although she is outside now clearing brush,† to try to get her back in here for one more time.

But okay, commentary. *Variety*'s review said that *Duck Soup* "has the Marxes madcapping thru such bits as the old Schwartz Bros. mirror routine, so well done in the hands of Groucho, Harpo and

---

* Not to mention *Las Meninas* and the "Mirror, Mirror" episode of *Star Trek*.
† Light brush, not chainsaw brush. I would not sit here idly watching a movie over and over while my wife toils as if she were a Republican president or a lumberjack.

Chico that it gathers a new and hilarious comedy momentum all over again." The only thing I have dug up on the Schwartz Brothers is a 1913 newspaper ad that shows them performing "The Broken Mirror" on a vaudeville bill including the Royal Jiu Jitsu Gladiators, Mado Minty "in her French spider speciality," and the Kauffman Family of bicycle riders. The Marxes may well have caught the Schwartz Brothers' act, or even shared a bill with it, but their mirror scene has movie roots as well.

In *The Hallucinations of Baron Munchausen* (1911), George Melies used a hollow frame with a lookalike performer and a mirror-image set behind it to create eerie illusions.

In *The Floorwalker* (1916), Charlie Chaplin is a bull-in-a-china-shop shopper who, in flight from detectives who think he is up to no good, runs into the store's office, where he encounters a man who looks pretty much exactly like him, except that his clothes aren't shabby. (He is the floorwalker, who was about to flee himself with a satchel of embezzled money.) Both men are dumbfounded. Moving in unison, they look each other over from head to toe, lean in closer, turn aside to scratch their heads, and so on. They reach out to touch hands, and then, spooked, they bolt in opposite directions. Then they reconsider, and exchange clothes and therefore identities. Much, much better than all this are Charlie's many entanglements with the store's escalator.

In *Seven Years Bad Luck* (1921), Max Linder plays a cook who pretends to be the master of the household's reflection, for seven minutes and thirty-two seconds, so the master won't discover that his valet has broken his new mirror. It helps that the master has awakened with a hangover. The illusion nearly breaks down when Linder has no shaving cream, just water, in his cup, so the master can't understand why he apparently has no shaving cream on his face. When the master turns to shout at the valet, Max quickly dips his brush into the master's cup and remedies the situation. But the master drops something, bends over, and turns around, and when he turns back, Max still has his butt pointed toward him. He's about to whack Max with his shoe—Max still doing his best to mimic him—when the phone rings in the next room. A lady friend invites him to come out, and while he's talking to her a new mirror is delivered, so when he returns and throws his shoe at what he thinks is Max, it smashes the mirror. You can see it on YouTube.

But the most germane predecessor to *Duck Soup*'s mirror scene, because it was directed by McCarey, is in *Mum's the Word* (1926). Charlie Chase slips out onto a second-story deck outside a bedroom so as not to be caught by a jealous husband, and when the husband sees Chase's shadow on the window shade, Chase imitates the husband's every move so that the husband will think he's seeing his own shadow. When the husband pulls out a cigarette and Chase can't come up with one, the husband sweeps aside the shade and there is Chase, offering him a light.

McCarey is generally given credit for suggesting the Marxes' version. Since *Duck Soup*, it has been copied by Abbott and Costello, by Tom (of Tom and Jerry) and another cat, by Bette Midler and herself playing the identical twin she didn't know she had, by David Niven and Robert Wagner wearing gorilla suits in *The Pink Panther*, and also, I am told, by characters in *The X-Files* and in several video games. These are just a few examples.

The best variations I have seen (they're both available online) are in cartoons. In *Lonesome Ghosts* (1937), Mickey Mouse, Donald Duck, and Goofy (who doesn't have a last name, does he? Goofy Dog?) are attempting, as proto-ghostbusters, to exorcise spirits from a house when Goofy looks into a dresser-top mirror and sees himself with the semitransparent face of a ghost. Goofy springs up and down, and the ghost springs with him. Goofy stops springing to fake the ghost out, but the ghost doesn't care, it keeps springing and grinning, which really puts Goofy off, so he dives into the mirror, smashes it, gets stuck, the ghost comes out through one of the drawers and grabs him by the feet, now Goofy's all wound up in the frame and the dresser drawers, he's wrestling with himself, choking his own neck, and his momentum carries this strange struggling amalgam of Goofy and dresser out the door and down the stairs, where it collides with Mickey and Donald and drives them into barrels of molasses and bags of flour, turning them into specters that scare away the real ghosts.

In *Hare Tonic* (1945), Elmer Fudd is carrying a basket with Bugs Bunny in it. Bugs sticks his head out and asks, "Whatcha got in the basket?"

"I have a wabbit. I'm gonna make a wabbit stew."

Bugs jumps out of the basket: "Hey, lemme see d' wabbit, Mister! Can I see d' wabbit, huh? Please let me see d' wabbit."

"All wight."

Bugs goes into the basket, comes out the other side. "No wabbit in there, Doc! You've been robbed!"

Elmer crawls into the basket himself, and Bugs starts carrying it—then Elmer realizes, "Oh, you twickster! *You're* the wabbit."

Elmer gets Bugs back in the basket, says he's going to take him home and make a stew of him.

Bugs, talking from the back of the basket: "He don't know me vewy well, do he?"

At Elmer's house, Bugs pretends to broadcast through the radio that people should beware of highly contagious rabbits with rabbititus—in advanced stages, sufferers assume the characteristics of rabbits.

This induces Elmer to throw Bugs out of the house, but that's not enough for Bugs: he returns. Introduces himself, in disguise, as a doctor. Elmer denies feeling "any rabbit inclinations."

"What's two times two?"

"Four."

"Aha! Multiplying!"

Then, having slid Elmer's mirror out of its frame, Bugs summons him to it and imitates his every movement, only in rabbit ways.

"I'm a wabbit!" cries Elmer.

In 1955, on *I Love Lucy,* Harpo and Lucille Ball, both dressed in Harpo outfits, re-created the *Duck Soup* mirror scene, sort of. They tried to do it before a studio audience, but couldn't get it together until many takes after the audience left. At first, Harpo kept adding new moves, apparently expecting Lucy to read his mind, and Lucy asked him to break it down into discrete bits of movement, which caused Harpo to start thinking, which made him lose track of what he was doing. Neither he nor Lucy was lissome anymore. They mainly succeeded in showing how much better Harpo and Groucho did it twenty-two years before.

The *New York Times* reviewer Mordaunt Hall, who found *Duck Soup* to be, "for the most part, extremely noisy without being nearly as mirthful as their other films," was such a close watcher that he identified the mirror scene's principals as Harpo and Chico, with Groucho coming in the end. That makes no sense on the face of it, since Harpo and Chico aren't trying to impersonate or fool each other—but it is unusual, in any of the movies, for Groucho and Harpo to pair off. When it's two brothers in a scene, it's almost always Chico and Harpo or Chico and Groucho. (I can't think of any scenes in which Chico is the only brother, except when he's playing the piano.) Chico and Harpo have a knockabout rapport, but the closest thing to an in-sync brotherly moment between Groucho and Harpo is in *A Night at the Opera* when Groucho demands of the villain, who is beating up on Harpo, "Hey, big bully, what's the idea of hitting that little bully?" This gives Harpo an opening to knock the villain out with a hammer. Then Harpo puts on a semiregretful face. "You're sorry for what you did, huh? That shows a nice spirit," says Groucho. Then Harpo hammers the villain again. Groucho and Harpo never come to fisticuffs, as Chico and Harpo do, but Groucho's usual response to Harpo is to look at him, cringe, and make a remark along the lines of this one in *A Night at the Opera:* "That's as grisly-a-looking object as I've ever seen."

Groucho and Harpo have a lot to work through. Groucho is the wiseacre, Harpo the mooncalf. Groucho the head, Harpo the soul, or something. In the mirror scene they establish that their bodies, at least, have a lot in common.

Here's a big difference between this mirror routine and the Max

Linder or the Charlie Chase or the Bugs and Elmer version: it is clear enough, about forty-nine seconds in, when we see the back of Groucho's head but his nodding, yeah-yeah, can't-fool-me expression is reflected by Harpo, that Groucho has, literally, not been fooled for a minute.* And yet he keeps on testing Harpo's illusionist chops for another two minutes and one second.

Why?

The purpose of acting, Hamlet informs the players, is "to hold, as 'twere, the mirror up to nature." As 'twere, indeed. The players might have answered, "Excuse us, Hamlet, but it seems like you've been trying to make nature be a mirror that you look justified in." Hilton Als, in the *New York Review*, writes that Michael Jackson saw in stardom "a chance to defend himself and his mother from the violent ministrations of his father . . . and to wrest from the world what most performers seek: a nonfractured mirroring."

Working well with another actor, actors say, has a mirroring effect: each player, by looking at the other's reactions, can get a fix on where he or she is, physically and emotively. On the other hand—as George Packer puts it[†]—there is "what's known in intelligence as 'mirror-imaging': seeing in an enemy's mental structure a reflection of one's own." Evidence-based imaging on the one hand, faith-based on the other. But the two are not mutually exclusive. If evidence can create faith, faith can also create evidence, and that's how the dark side is born.

---

* A question sometimes raised: what happened to all the broken glass? The technical answer: someone in the crew swept it up between shots.
† Packer, in the *New Yorker*, was accusing Republicans of projecting aims of "tyranny" upon Barack Obama—who, I would say, as of this writing, has turned out to display far less in the way of Marxian high-handedness than many, on the left and the right, had hoped.

This is not so much a movie about how nations go to war as it is about something deeper—the way brothers fight, compulsively, appetitively, because they can't help it. As they grow on each other they grow over against each other. They get in each other's way, they pick on each other, they put each other down, they look for excuses to regard each other as threats—thereby acquiring moves not taught in the classroom but essential, if not necessarily salubrious, in life. Brothers, usually, don't quite kill each other, but they do know each other perhaps better than either would like. The Marx Brothers, when not in differing costumes, strikingly resembled each other. Once Harpo went on the panel quiz show *I've Got a Secret,* answering questions with horn honks. Turned out, his secret was that he was Chico pretending to be Harpo. In *Animal Crackers,* Groucho tells Chico he used to know someone who looked just like him, named Emanuel Ravelli. "Are you his brother?"

Chico says he is Emanuel Ravelli.

"Well," says Groucho, "no wonder you look like him. But I still insist, there is a resemblance."

Chico laughs. "Hey, he thinks I look alike."

More fraught than Chico's resemblance to himself is the relationship between Groucho and Harpo. Here (in nighty-night outfits that make them look like little kids) we have the brooding, dark brother vis-à-vis the buoyant, faux-blond brother. The brother who was playing a German in the family act, until the *Lusitania* was sunk—"So I became a Jew comedian. I never was a Jew comedian before"—vis-à-vis the brother who played silent Irish. The brother of the sidelong looks vis-à-vis the brother who made goony head-on faces. The brother whose mother didn't like him vis-à-vis the brother who was most like her. Two brothers who didn't hang out together as kids and—though Groucho's son said the only time he ever saw his father cry was when Harpo died—were probably not much at ease with each other as grown-ups either, except when performing.

"You love your brother, don't you?" Groucho asks Chico, as regards Harpo, in *Go West*.

"No, but I'm used to him," says Chico.

Groucho and Harpo in the mirror routine are truly, madly, deeply used to each other.

True bromance entails respect and kinesthetic empathy, but also intense competition. This match between Harpo and Groucho is a lot like basketball. "You've got to try and anticipate a little bit," says former Orlando Magic player Courtney Lee about guarding the Lakers' Kobe Bryant. "But you don't want to anticipate too much. He has that great footwork, and you can think he's going one way, and he'll feel you and make the right pivot and go the other way." Groucho and Chico are working together, but this still must have been a hard thing to pull off. And between their characters, it is a duel.

Harpo, so often put down by Groucho in words, keeps winning this face-off. He can cover Groucho—can *be* Groucho, to all appearances, when he wants to. When Groucho does a spin move, Harpo doesn't even whirl around, because he knows Groucho can't see him when he's facing away.* When Groucho thinks he's got him this time, different hats, Harpo switches hats.

But Groucho never loses his cool. Firefly is failing to fake out Pinky, but Groucho the bookworm is matching his loosey-goosey brother move for move. When Harpo slips up and drops his hat,

---

* This move inspired Gene Kelly to pull a similar one in his dancing-with-himself scene in *Cover Girl*.

Groucho graciously hands it back to him, and they exchange a little bow. Groucho is no Edgar Kennedy—he *gets* this new take on tit-for-tat. He's mulling a new move when Chico bursts in and the one-on-one is over.

Harpo gets away. Groucho grabs Chico, who will be tried for treason.

This courtroom scene is the one T. S. Eliot, a big fan, wanted to discuss when Groucho visited him in London. Groucho demurred—he wanted to discuss *Murder in the Cathedral*. Eliot demurred.

The prosecutor is Charles Middleton, who had played Abraham Lincoln in a short film promoting the aforementioned National Recovery Act. More notably, he would go on to play Ming the Merciless in the "Flash Gordon" serial. His grandfather, Arthur Middleton, had signed the Declaration of Independence. His grandson, Burr Middleton, would play "Sleazy Photographer" in *Goodbye, Norma Jean*.

Chico objects.

"On what grounds?" asks the prosecutor.

"I couldn't think of anything else to say," says Chico. And Groucho can't think of anything else either. So often in life those grounds must suffice.

Listen to Groucho saying, "Look at Chicolini. He sits there alone." Just that part. Doesn't that sound like Homer Simpson's voice when he is pitying himself? Dan Castellaneta, who does Homer's voice, has said that he based Homer's trademark *d'oh* on the slow-burn ejaculation of James Finlayson, who often played the Edgar Kennedy foil for Laurel and Hardy when they weren't playing it for each other. So, I'm just saying, Castellaneta might have been trolling around for vintage comic voice tones and picked up on this one.

If you don't have the French subtitles up, I'll bet you're wondering how Chicolini's famous *irrelevant/elephant* pun plays in that language. It's *hors de propos* and *hippopo*. French for *irrelevant* and *hippo*. A hippo has *un tronc mais pas de feuilles*—a trunk in the sense of torso/tree, but no leaves. Pretty clever. Less felicitous is the replacement of Chicolini's other famous pun on *lemonade/eliminate* by a confusion of *omettre* (omit) and *omelette*. But how would you like to translate Chicolini into another language? Even pseudo-Italian.

Trentino is coming back, one last peace effort. Great idea, says Firefly, he'll be glad to reach out himself. But in a flash it hits him what a downer that would be. It is so much more *rousing* to imagine that when he reaches out to the peace seeker, the peace seeker will refuse to accept, which will be a humiliation that no Firefly can tolerate. So when the peace seeker arrives, Groucho has at him again with his trusty glove. A remark by the late Dan May, businessman and philosopher of Nashville, Tennessee, may be apropos here: "There is one thing and one thing only that will create a sudden war at any time, and that is a conviction that we are appeasers."

This means war! All righty then!

But first let us pause to consider the structure of *Duck Soup*. According to standard screenwriting theory, a movie must consist of three acts. One: thirty minutes of setup, including an "inciting incident" that causes the hero to take on the problem. Two: an hour of complications leading to another key plot point that causes a reversal. Three: thirty more minutes of resolution.

You *might* say that act 1 of *Duck Soup* is its first thirty minutes, culminating in the first time Groucho insults Trentino, at the garden party. Act 2 would then be the skulduggery involving the plans and the mirror, ending in Groucho's third insult of Trentino. And act 3 is the forthcoming fifteen minutes of war. Where's the "reversal"? Nowhere. *Duck Soup* is ineluctably headed for war from the get-go. *Duck Soup* is subversive of standard screenwriting theory.

One more look at what's in the Kalmar-Ruby script:

> An exploding Zeppelin. Would have been a bit over the top.
> And not character-driven, even if the Zeppelin were taken
> to represent Zeppo.

> Harpo driving his motorcycle through a trench, soldiers
> leaping out of his way all along. A good enough idea
> that it was filmed: seven years later, in *The Bank Dick,* W. C.
> Fields drove a car through a ditch, ditch diggers jumping out
> all along.

> Get this, a reconciliatory postwar banquet.
> *All wrong, all wrong.*

No, Freedonia *wants* to go to war. "*At last* we're going to war." Because a movie needs a dramatic climax, and because so do people, alas. "This is a fact we can't ignore." This movie has momentum because it is about what people at their worst (well, not *worst* worst, no torture or genocide) take a hankering to do.

Freedonians are *writhing* in the *ecstasy* of anticipating war.

Harpo reappears as a drum major. And here comes the clip that gives the Woody Allen character Mickey reason to live, back in 1986, in *Hannah and Her Sisters*.

For some reason, Mickey has been hung up on the question, if there is no God or afterlife, why is this life worth living? To me that is like asking: why eat lunch if there's nothing for dinner? But Mickey has gone so far in his spiritual quest as to consider and reject both Catholicism (thereby missing an opportunity for some great Jewish-Irish syzygy, with Cardinal O'Connor still alive—or Bill Murray could have had a cameo as either a Bing or a Barry Fitzgerald padre) and Hare Krishna. Mickey is so hung up on the purpose of life that he has just now tried ambivalently to shoot himself and missed. Shocked by his own "violent and unreal" behavior, he wan-

McCarey saves an unidentified damsel from Harpo with shears meant for plume snipping.

ders into an Upper West Side movie theater, the Metro,* hoping to "put the world back into rational perspective." And the next thing we see is the four Marxes turning soldiers' heads into a xylophone and Harpo snipping off the soldiers' plumes, to the beat.

That's some droll montage. You'd think the next shot would be of Mickey dancing ecstatically in the balcony there, with other patrons yelling at him to sit down. But we have no sense that there is anyone else in the audience, certainly no hint of laughter. Instead of dancing, Mickey thinks. In voice-over, he reasons with himself, as the brothers swing into *hidey-hidey-ho* and so on. God help us, Mickey *is* looking to the Marx Brothers for rational perspective.

"Look at all those people on the screen," says Mickey, who has seen this movie many times since childhood and loves it. "They're real funny." As we cut back and forth between a musing Mickey and a screen full of people standing on their hands kicking both feet in the air by way of acting out war fever, Mickey comes around finally to deciding that he'll reserve judgment about God (could I get, from above, a sigh of relief?) and enjoy life. "How can you even think of killing yourself, I mean, isn't it so stupid?"

I'd say so, yes, unless you're in a good deal more agony than Mickey has the chops to convey. Can we imagine the reverse case, of any Marx brother finding a reason to live in *Hannah and Her Sisters*? Groucho was a big fan of Woody Allen, though, and the way his old crush Maureen O'Sullivan plays Hannah's salty mother might have reminded him of Minnie. Lloyd Nolan as her father is maybe a little like Frenchie. And Hannah's sisters, played engagingly by Barbara Hershey and Dianne Wiest, might suggest Harpo

---

* It's empty now, but still standing—they couldn't tear it down for a condo, because it's art deco.

(free spirit) and Groucho (neurotic), respectively. But that would leave Chico as the over-responsible Hannah, played tightly by Mia Farrow, who was Allen's life companion at the time. Let's move on from *Hannah and Her Sisters*. I just watched the big reconciled-family Thanksgiving scene at the end and realized that the cute little girl who greets the Wiest character at the door must be Farrow's adopted daughter Soon-yi Previn (uncredited), here looking younger than her age (twelve), now the Woodman's wife.

The Marx Brothers were not military types. When the United States entered World War I, Minnie found out that producers of food were draft-deferred, so she set the boys up in a chicken farm. They were not agricultural types either. They couldn't stop rats from eating all the eggs, so when a customer or curious visitor was expected, they would run into town and buy eggs to put in the nests. Near the end of the war, Gummo did get drafted, which is why Zeppo had to give up a life of crime, but Gummo served his country by introducing officers to chorus girls in Chicago.

"And then the war came," said Groucho on the radio many years later, "and I fought all the way. But I hadda go anyway."

No, he didn't, thanks to Minnie. So *Duck Soup*'s disrespect for war was not inspired by traumatic experience in the trenches, nor, it would appear, by Groucho's devotion to the Irving Berlin song about brothers being turned into butchers. What we have here is war as a handy hook on which to hang as many violations of traditional music as can be worked into one propulsive number. The *hidey-ho* business, which I guess you could call jazz-inflected, flows into the lamentational "Woe-oh-woe," which flows into the remarkably upbeat desecration of a Negro spiritual, "They got guns, we got guns, all God's chillun got guns," with

Groucho going all bobblehead and Harpo all bobble-bodied, and then, slick as a whistle (the camera panning away, for a change, and then back), the boys have picked up banjos, and before you know it we're all in a hoedown, with Harpo high-shit-kicking as only he can and Groucho doing something like the opposite of his trademark walk—he's leading with his knees instead of his head, he's stiff-backed and bent-kneed, as if he's dancing tied to a chair, and somehow it makes him look downright rural. Then suddenly the gravity of the situation hits everyone for about five seconds until Harpo gets them back on track by playing "Turkey in the Straw" on a fiddle, and they're square dancing again, but Harpo has lost his fiddle bow, seems he has stuck it in his butt somehow.

It's the only time in a movie that all four boys played music together. One thing that is so appealing about this segment of Zeppo's last movie is that he and the other three boys are equally involved, having a fine old time together. No reason for anybody to feel left out. In the early forties, Ben Hecht got several Hollywood people, including Harpo and the composer George Antheil, together to play chamber music. Groucho wanted to lend his talents on the mandolin, but was rebuffed on the grounds that his instrument wasn't dignified enough. The group had just begun their first rehearsal at Hecht's house, upstairs, when there was a loud banging on the door of the room and the uninvited Groucho flung it open.

"Quiet, please!" he shouted, then slammed the door behind him.

"Groucho's jealous," Harpo explained. The group began to play again. Once again Groucho burst in, shouting, "Quiet, you lousy amateurs!" After an awkward pause, he slammed the door again.

Then, as the group resumed their rehearsal, they heard, from downstairs, at great volume, the overture to *Tannhäuser*.

Antheil recalled that the group was "thunderstruck. We all crawled down the stairway to look. There was Groucho, directing, with great batlike gestures, the Los Angeles Symphony Orchestra. At least one hundred men had been squeezed into the living room. Groucho had hired them." Okay. Groucho was allowed to join the Ben Hecht Symphonietta.

In "To War . . . ," sibling rivalry rises to revelry. Where do we go from there? We go to the solo midnight ride of Harpo. Another nightmare for Edgar Kennedy. Harpo's got to mobilize the citizenry against invaders, but wouldn't you know he'd ride past a window and see a blonde in her undies? And wouldn't you know whose wife she is?

In *At the Circus*, Harpo manages to get inside the mattress of an ill-natured strongman while the latter is trying to sleep on it. In the famous stateroom scene in *A Night at the Opera*, Harpo winds up limply asleep on a large tray that waiters have used to serve food. And we have seen Harpo get into Edgar Kennedy's pocket and his lemonade. But to come up, fully dressed and blowing a bugle, from underneath an Irish-American man in his own bathtub!

Duty calls, Harpo's body language expresses rather more eloquently than necessary, and he's off to alert the nation. It's a tough job, but it's okay because Harpo finds another lady in another window, and—didn't I tell you Marxes don't get the girl? Maybe they would if Judd Apatow were directing, but he isn't.

Harpo winds up, by preference, in bed with the horse. A note here: McCarey supervised a Laurel and Hardy, called *Wrong Again,* in which a horse winds up standing on a piano, and the Harold Lloyd vehicle *The Milky Way,* in which Lloyd loads a young horse into the back of a taxi. In the latter case the colt would not vocalize, so McCarey did the whinnies, and they were so convincing that he left them in.*

Okay, last time we saw Groucho he was posing heroically in the uniform of a revolutionary patriot. Now he's in, I don't know what uniform, maybe Civil War or Zouave, and his aides are in something like World War I Prussian. They're under bombardment, and the enemy has seized certain hills, "throwing thirteen hillbillies out of work." Want to know what French for "hillbillies" is? *Péquenauds.* Not in my French dictionary. We should all watch this with a French person sometime. Maybe you are a French person! Watch it with a hillbilly!

Sometimes Groucho's jokes seem almost pointedly thematic:

"Any answer to that message?"

"No, sir."

"Well, in that case, don't send it."

That thinking is a lot like the thinking that finally got Freedonia into this war: welcoming an opportunity to extend the right hand of good fellowship, but what if he doesn't take it how will that make me look so instead slap him with the right hand of paranoia.

What is Groucho satirizing? The insecurity that gives rise to warmongering, or his own insecurity? Why not both?

The French for "this is the last straw" is evidently *c'est la goutte d'eau qui fait deborder le vase,* which I'm going to go ahead and

---

* During the filming of *The Milky Way,* by the way, McCarey was poisoned by some bad milk.

translate as "this is the drop of water that makes the vase overflow." The French translator would seem to have thrown in the towel.

Zeppo informs Groucho that he's shooting his own men. After shooting some more of them, Groucho takes this on board, offers to bribe Zeppo to keep it secret, then takes the money back. Some viewers, I have read, are put off by this. But for one thing, *c'est la guerre,* and for another thing, as Buster Keaton said of the Marxes, "Pathos had nothing to do with them. They never even got into a situation where you'd feel sorry for anybody." That's true at least when they are really cooking, when the romantic subplot isn't dragging them in. "Course, they'd kid themselves in and out of everything," said Keaton. Yes. They are kids. They kid. They give each other, and everybody else, a hard time. That didn't go over so well in hard times evidently. But that is their heroism. The kids I was watching the movie with at the Thalia were eating this up.

Now Groucho is in a Confederate uniform. And Chicolini pops in. When last seen, he was being tried for treason against Freedonia. Since then he has apparently re-upped as Freedonian Secretary of War, because now he's done something about the fact that Freedonia is losing the war—he's quite frankly gone over (again) to the other side, but the food is better over here—have I lost track of this sentence? What matters is, all the boys are back together.

And whom have we been missing? Here she is, Mrs. T!

Groucho greets her as a uniformed Boy Scout. You can see by Harpo's outfit that he is an admiral, or something, employed at the moment as a rifleman. Another cut, and it's Groucho in a stupendous busby and a snappy frogged-front jacket. Another one, and Groucho is in Davy Crockett garb, and Zeppo is seizing the opportunity, at last, to show off how buff his upper body is.

Someone's got to go for help. A kid's ritual to choose who's it. Chico cheats, so Harpo's it. Must have happened all the time in their boyhood. "And remember, when you're out there risking life and limb . . . we'll be in here thinking what a sucker you are." An unpalatable sentiment if I ever heard one. Those kids I was watching with at the Thalia—kids who knew from siblings—were eating it up.

You *know* Harpo had to cut Groucho's coontail off. The tail was there, the scissors were there. Master's theses have no doubt been devoted to Harpo and . . . whatever it's called, psychologically, I forget here now in the heat of battle, when brothers cut tails off brothers.

Help is on the way . . . Never before or since in the history of

Firefly as angel of mercy? No wonder this was cut.

cinema has there been such a spontaneous outpouring of stock footage: firetrucks, motorcycle cops, distance runners, rowers, swimmers, baboons and stampeding elephants (clipped from the great semi-documentary *Chang,* by Merion Cooper, the primary creator of *King Kong*), and last but not least, dolphins. Dolphins not frolicking as these aquatic mammals are wont to do but coursing determinedly toward our side (we're Freedonia) by sea.

And look here. Far from going all tony and wilting on us in a pinch, Mrs. T is right there at the barricade, in couture by Molly Pitcher, loading rifles for the boys. And now that Groucho has his head caught in a chamber pot (to a wartime president, things happen), she's firing a rifle herself.* And she's helping to hold the door against a battering ram—but there's a rearguard line to be drawn as well: "Oh, don't touch me! Keep away from me!" (*Ne me touchez pas! Laissez-moi tranquille!*) has the heartfelt ring of Maggie Dumont speaking ad-lib for herself. She *will not* have horrid Harpo help her by placing both hands firmly on her ass.

Freedonia has captured Trentino, his head jammed into the broken door! What a perfect opportunity to throw fruit at someone. Someone on the other side even.

The *u*-word is still stuck in Groucho's craw: "Call me an upstart, eh?"

---

* She may have shot Groucho in the butt accidentally, which led to his calling for water and his being crowned with a chamber pot, but that is not entirely clear. Note that big brother Chico is the only Marx who—with help from little brother Zeppo, who probably could have done the job himself—actually dispatches an enemy soldier coming over the top. Conks him on the head with something—a brick? Where do you come up with a brick in a moment like that? Maybe growing up the way Chico did, you keep a brick for emergencies. If you click your way through this sequence frame by frame, by the way, it looks for all the world like something from *All Quiet on the Western Front* except for Groucho with the pot on his head.

And the Marxes run to the throwable fruit.

Freeze a moment, if you will, for a few words about artful throwing. Hear the great and fastidious silent craftsman Buster Keaton lay this down:

> For one we don't use a regular baker's pie, and throwing the pie in a cardboard plate is no good because that plate flying off detracts. So, what we used to do is our prop man would get our baker . . . to make pie crust, two of them, with nothing in them, and take just a little flour and water to make a paste, just enough to glue the two together. That was so that your fingers wouldn't go through the bottom of it. Now you fill it, about an inch, with just flour and water mixed, which clings like glue and stretches. Now, on top of it, if I'm going to hit somebody in dark clothes, a brunette, you put a lemon meringue type of topping to it and garnish with whipped cream, you see. When it was a light costume, a blond, something like that, you put in blueberry and then enough whipped cream just to spatter.

Keaton once threw a pie twenty-seven feet, he says, and "caught the villain plum in the puss with it."

The Marxes are not that old-school. In this, the last gasp of *Duck Soup*, they throw fruit from close range. What kind of fruit is unclear. It would appear to be some kind of stage fruit. It is round. It bounces gratifyingly enough off Trentino's nose. It does not smash. The throwing rather than splatter is the thing.

All four boys, throwing together. One day, decades before, Minnie had booked Harpo, Groucho, and Gummo's act "Skule

Days" into Waukegan, Illinois. Harpo, as he recalled in *Harpo Speaks!,* was doing some bit of business involving an orange and a hat when he looked into the orchestra pit and "let out a whoop." He threw the orange at the guy playing the piano, who threw it back. When Groucho and Gummo looked, they whooped too. "We heaved everything we could get our hands on into the orchestra pit—hats, books, chalk, erasers, stilettos. The piano player surrendered. He climbed up onto the stage . . . and joined the act. It was Chico."

Chico, who had been traveling independently, playing the piano for gambling money, had found himself in Waukegan on the same day as his family and had bribed their regular pianist to let him sit in. From then on, Chico was a brother not only by blood but also onstage. And Chico took over management of the act from Minnie and the act evolved into brotherly war.

So.

Why is it so gratifying that as soon as Mrs. T pipes up with "Victory is owahs!" and starts to sing, quite suitably one would think, the Freedonian national anthem—why is it so gratifying that the boys turn and start throwing at her? You don't find it gratifying?

Why is it so gratifying to me, then? And why was it so gratifying to that audience of contemporary children and young parents and nannies with whom I was watching *Duck Soup* at the Thalia? Why is it so *climactically* gratifying for the boys to turn and start throwing their fruit at poor, gallant Mrs. T? Who is *on their side*! Who is the figurehead of their ship of state. A nice proper lady who loves them (or anyway loves Groucho, the least lovable) and who, by the way, is bankrolling this whole war.

Are they throwing at Mom? A mother who, in the Marxes'

case, deprived them of a normal childhood by pushing them onto the stage? Nah. Where would they have found a normal childhood at the time and in the place where they grew up? And what would they have done with a normal childhood? Less, surely, than what they did with the childhood they had.

Are they throwing at Collectivism? We don't know whether Freedonia's economy will ever rebound, but we do know, now, that it wasn't the New Deal alone that pulled America out of the Depression. It took World War II.

Are they throwing at Fascism? The report that Benito Mussolini took the movie personally and banned it in Italy has the ring of studio publicity. (The mayor of Fredonia, New York, did protest *Duck Soup*, just before its premiere, as a blot on his town's fair name, but that was a put-up deal, enabling Groucho's public response: "Change the name of your town, it's hurting our movie.") Another classic film that came out in 1933 was *Zero for Conduct*, French, directed by Jean Vigo. Schoolboys in revolt against their school. *Zero for Conduct* bears some eerie resemblances to *Duck Soup*:

> Its protagonists are three rebellious boys and a new boy who becomes their fourth.

> During the film's most celebrated scene, the pillow fight, the boys are in white nightgowns and the sound track goes from a raucous score to spooky silence.

> There is a remarkable hat-and-mirror scene in which the headmaster, a dwarf, is at great pains to position his hat on a mantelpiece, and then we see a mirror, and the headmaster starts straightening his tie, as if in the

mirror over the mantel—but he's too short to show up in the mirror, so a tall man standing behind him serves as his reflection, standing back (we see him alone in the mirror), straightening his own tie, smoothing his own hair as, presumably, the headmaster does, then sitting down as the headmaster does.

Two of the boys bow to each other remarkably like Groucho and Harpo in their mirror routine.

The film moves not according to plot logic but—ineluctably—more like a dream.

The boys smoke cigars.

The boys and a sympathetic teacher chase after an attractive woman in the street, inconclusively, like Harpo.

That teacher does a drawing that becomes magically animated, like Harpo's tattoo. And he does funny walks, like Groucho.

The boys smash dishes with the abandon of Harpo wielding his scissors.

The boys mock war. ("It's war! Down with school! Liberty or death!")

The movie is even shorter than *Duck Soup,* only fifty minutes.

The movie ends with the four boys throwing things (garbage, from the roof) at stuffed shirts.

Zero for Conduct came out in time—April of '33—to have influenced *Duck Soup*. But it was shown only in France, and only to small audiences there, before being suppressed. Could Mankiewicz, say, have caught a screening of it? Unlikely. Maybe there was something in the international atmosphere, under whose pressure both movies bubbled up.

Say both movies were responses, at some level, to looming totalitarianism. *Zero for Conduct* had a distinctly political heritage. Jean Vigo's father was a famous anarchist who took the name Almereyda, an anagram of *y a la merdre** ("there is shit"), and was strangled in prison when Jean was twelve. Jean himself died in 1934, leaving a few films so oddly put together that they would not be appreciated until many years later. But *Zero for Conduct*, for all its elements of farce, is rationally, pointedly anarchic, a protest against the hypocritical, unjust authority. The freedom-loving, uncorrupted boys are the good guys, the stiffs are repressive, predatory grotesques. We are frightened for the boys. They have feelings. They are able to form sympathetic alliances. At the end you sort of want to say, Aww. Unless you have totalitarian sympathies, in which case you're presumably saying, *Get those boys off that roof and into a camp.*

The Marxes and McCarey, in conflict, in Hollywood, on the pre-Code cusp between silent and screwball, managed to make a movie more uncompromisingly anarchic than that French art film. Everybody in *Duck Soup*, except maybe Miss Vera Marcal and sometimes Zeppo, is grotesque. There is no one to feel sorry for, not even Mrs. T. "The Marxes revolt against kindly Margaret Dumont," observes

---

* The very interesting contemporary American director Michael Almereyda (see his *Hamlet*, with Ethan Hawke in the title role and Bill Murray as Polonius) assumed that name with the anagram in mind.

Raymond Durgnat, "because, through our comic heroes, we sense the smothering quality of such 'niceness.'"

In l933 Europeans should have been so lucky as to be smothered by niceness. But after *Duck Soup* the Marxes got nicer themselves, in movies, alas. When asked what *Duck Soup* was up to, Groucho always insisted, "We were just four Jews trying to be funny." But so were they in their later movies. In *Duck Soup* they manage to have it both ways—they are solidly in charge, yet thoroughly insurgent. Maybe that combination of rooted and rebellious is, or was, the American dream.

Let's say they are liberty personified, throwing at Miss Liberty, as represented by statuesque Mrs. T. Are they making a statement to the effect that liberty, by its nature, will turn on you if you try to set it in concrete? Nah. Liberty is not to be set in statement either.

But we can freeze liber*ties,* on film. That's what I'm doing now—examining the pelting of Mrs. T frame by frame. Look carefully, and what do you see hanging slightly downstage of her and just to her right?

A noose.

"Victory is ow-ahs!" she flutes (or rather, oboes) with right arm raised, and indeed she does evoke Madame Liberty, for all her lack of a torch. And she begins to sing, operatically, "Hail, hail . . ."

And the boys turn and begin to pelt her. My grandsons would love to have some of those prop fruits—apparently denser than Nerf but softer than tennis balls. I like to think they wouldn't throw them at Margaret Dumont.

But look! The boys *aren't* throwing at her! They're throwing at the noose! There's your answer, Alvy Singer, there's the purpose of life: to throw things at death!

Or maybe McCarey, their romantic director, has told them: we don't want to hit Maggie, of course, we'll cheat it—aim at the noose.

But then Harpo hits the noose. And they do start throwing at her. If we wonder why McCarey had such negative things to say about *Duck Soup*—he was a sentimental Irishman. He would go on to direct some of the fondest mother scenes ever on film. In *Going My Way*, tottery Barry Fitzgerald's ancient, even-more-tottery mother, whom he hasn't seen in God knows how many years, arrives, surprise!, from the mother country and takes him to her bosom. He's retiring, belatedly, but he's still her baby. It doesn't get any less like throwing fruit at a doting older lady than that.

" . . . Freedonia, *laaaand* of the *braaav*"—that's as far as Maggie gets, and it looks like Chico at the end has gone back to targeting the noose, but the others have Mrs. T fending off projectiles with both hands (at one point she appears to catch one with her left hand, whereupon it melts—but that's an illusion*) as we close. War blown away. Happy endings scorned. Triumphalism trumped.

"We didn't care about defending Freedonia," Groucho once explained. "We just liked throwing things."

R eviews were mixed, and the movie was much less profitable than the Marxes' earlier ones. The *Los Angeles Times*, January 1, 1934: "Every indication points to the Marx Brothers' being through with the movies for the time being. They played the game for what it was worth but the screen is relentless in its exac-

---

* Like everything else in movies.

tions on comedians. It's their duty to be funnier in each succeeding picture . . .

"Groucho Marx dropped the word in New York that they've finished up for the time being. It looks like a stage show, and then maybe back to Paramount." But Paramount was in receivership. On the radio, someone asked Groucho why he wanted to make movies anyway. "The movies is classy," he said.

His scapegrace eldest brother stepped up. Many years later, Irving Brecher, who wrote the screenplays of *At the Circus* and *Go West,* related Groucho's version of Chico's intervention. It seems that Al Lichtman, the head of distribution at MGM, was a fellow member of the Hillcrest Country Club. Lichtman considered himself a gin rummy player. "Everybody says you're the best at the club," he said to Chico. "Me, I don't think so."

"I'm lucky," said Chico. "I win, I lose . . ."

Lichtman suggested they go head to head. Chico shrugged okay. Kibitzers gathered. Chico lost a few hundred dollars. Said he had no money on him. Lichtman: "No problem. See you tomorrow."

The next day, even more onlookers, even more gin. Chico lost almost a thousand. Told Lichtman he still didn't have the money on him. Lichtman said not to worry.

Next day, Chico suggested doubling the stakes, give him a chance to catch up. Lichtman readily agreed. Before an even larger crowd, Chico lost and lost, until he was down sixty-eight hundred. Lichtman asked him, gentleman to gentleman, whether this was not the point at which he should pay up. Chico was close to tears. Not only did he lack the cash, he confessed, he was about to go bankrupt, because the Marxes had no movie in the works. "If we were doing a movie, then I could pay you, of course."

Lichtman was magnanimous. "Just remember to tell everybody who's the best gin player in the club." Chico gave him a big grateful hug.

A couple of days later, Chico answered the phone, and it was Zeppo, now the brothers' agent. Zeppo was excited: "Out of the blue, I got a call from MGM."

"Who over there?" asked Chico.

"Al Lichtman. He recommended to Thalberg that they sign us up, and Thalberg okayed it."

The brothers converged on the offices of Irving Thalberg, head of production at MGM. "The Boy Genius," as he was called, wasn't there when they arrived. What, *he* was going to keep *them* waiting? When he showed up, they were in his inner office, naked, roasting potatoes over a fire in his fireplace.

Okay, down to brass tacks. Without Zeppo, Thalberg argued, they should get less money. "Without Zeppo," said Groucho, "we're twice as funny." Zeppo negotiated a five-picture deal.

At the club, Chico thanked Lichtman. "Wanna celebrate?" said Lichtman. "Let's play some gin."

Okay, said Chico. In three hours, nobody watching much, he won back the $6,800 and a little extra.

"Let's make them lovable," said Thalberg. "Pictures," he had written, "should be made primarily for the feminine mind." In their first movie under Thalberg, *A Night at the Opera*, the Marxes run riot through grand opera, but for a good cause: to advance the romance and the singing careers of lovesongbirds Kitty Carlisle and Alan Jones. Bleh.

Opera also had great comedy. The famous full-to-bursting stateroom scene. Groucho and Chico going over a contract, progressively reducing it to a single shred. The strenuous injection of "Take Me Out to the Ball Game" (the song and a bit of the game itself) into *Il Trovatore*. The movie made a lot of money. It was no *Duck Soup*. In 2009, by the way, according to a website called FemaleFirst, British schoolchildren who were shown a series of classic films voted *Duck Soup* their number-one favorite, ahead of *The Wizard of Oz, Bambi, It's a Wonderful Life, Dumbo* . . .

Thalberg died. The Marxes grew older. The romantic subplots grew sappier. Their madness went downhill.

O n the Internet, it is often stated that François Truffaut called *Duck Soup* the most effective, or the only valid, antiwar movie ever made. But our heroes *bring on* the war—the bad guy tries to avert it. They *enjoy* the war. And they *win* the war. Only then do they seem to be turning against it. But there is no indication that they wouldn't happily start another war tomorrow.

An antiwar movie is *The Bridge on the River Kwai*, whose last word is "Madness!" but before that you get some noble self-sacrifice and a really cool explosion that sends a bad-guy bridge and a bad-guy train full of bad guys spilling down into the river. What Truffaut did say was in response to the question (posed to him by Robert Hughes), "Which of the films dealing with peace, and war, do you think are the most effective?"

"It seems to me," replied Truffaut, "that war films, even pacifist, even the best, willingly or not, glorify war and render it in some way attractive: *La Grande Illusion* (which I admire) makes one want to be a prisoner; *Paisan* (which I admire) to be a partisan; *Le*

Petit Soldat (which I admire) to become a secret agent; and *Sergeant York* (which I admire) a war hero.

"A film that truly shows war, battles, almost necessarily exalts war unless it is a question of a parody: *Shoulder Arms, Tire au Plane* (by Jean Renoir), *Duck Soup, The Great Dictator*."

I haven't seen *Tire au Plane*, but Renoir himself remarked ruefully of *La Grande Illusion*, "In 1937 I was told I had made the greatest antiwar picture—two years later war broke out." Of the other three parodies Truffaut cites, *Duck Soup* is the least beholden, the most defiant. Defiant not just of war but of pacifism, of fellow feeling, of *movies*, of everything. This comedy made in the same year that Hitler became chancellor of Germany is not, like *The Great Dictator* of seven years later, an attempt to send up a fuehrer. "The fact of the matter," wrote George F. Kennan, "is that there is a little bit of the totalitarian buried somewhere, way down deep, in each and every one of us." If only you could be a dictator without the headaches . . .

You'd be Firefly, for whom everything is duck soup, except when his even more blithely despotic big brothers are around. *Time* magazine, calling the recent comedies of Will Ferrell "macho infantilism," suggested their popularity might reflect "that inside every adult is a backward child ruled by fears and cravings," or just that audiences like "grownups behaving . . . like kindergartners making poop jokes." Either way, too cutesy: buck up, little stinky man. *Duck Soup* is more radical. In the "Going to war!" number, all of a sudden Zeppo sings, "Oh how we'd cry / For Firefly / If Firefly should die!" Yeah, right. *Duck Soup* is a feel-good movie with no concession—not even way down deep, not even off in the wings somewhere—to obligatory feeling.

> **CHICO:** Ya gotta admit, it's brave
> and free, donia?

It *is* sort of sweet that all the brothers unite there at the end. Should say, most of the brothers. Here's something I did not know until I read Sally Ashley's biography of Franklin P. Adams, who was a prominent figure at the legendarily witty Algonquin Round Table. According to that book, only one Marx contributed an unforgotten pun to the Round Tablers' vaunted word games. It wasn't Groucho, who must have been furious. Nor was it Harpo, who for all we know sat at the table naked. Nor was it Chico, who had more dangerous games elsewhere.

It was Gummo. Evidently Gummo had a seat at that table at least

LEFT TO RIGHT: *Harpo, Zeppo, Chico, Groucho, and Gummo, 1957.*

once, and he made it count. Everybody knows that Dorothy Parker, challenged to make a sentence with the word *horticulture,* quipped as follows: "You can lead a horticulture, but you can't make her think." But who knew that Gummo, taking on *euphoria,* came up with this:

"Go outside and play," Minnie told the brothers.

"Which ones?" they asked.

And she said: "Euphoria."*

---

* If Gummo is included, that leaves Zeppo out again. In his seventies, Zeppo fell for a cook employed by Groucho. She was extremely young and also extremely tall, especially compared to Zeppo. "What do you want from her?" Groucho demanded. "Whatever I can reach," said Zeppo. "What good to you are her *feet*?" said Groucho.

Photo Credits

Roy Blount Jr. is the author of twenty-one previous books, most recently *Alphabet Juice*. He appears regularly on NPR's *Wait, Wait . . . Don't Tell Me* and is a member of the Fellowship of Southern Writers. He lives in western Massachusetts.